A PEMBROKESHIRE PENTACLE

by

GEORGE W H JACKSON

INTRODUCTION

A pentacle is a five pointed star and in this book the undoubted star is Pembrokeshire itself. The five points of that star are the five incarnations in which I came to know and love that County.

First as a holidaymaker, then as a police officer serving in both Milford Haven and my own patch covering Dale, Marloes and St Ishmaels followed by a spell as an office administrator working in Haverfordwest with the Herald Bard of Wales and finally as Landlord of the Brook Inn at St Ishmaels and Town Clerk in Pembroke.

The lure of the place was such that one of my two sisters, my parents and my brother all moved to Pembrokeshire as well. These are my memories of the people, places and events during the period 1967-84 which were such an important and enjoyable part of my life.

My thanks are due to all those members of my family who have helped me to recall memories many of which they helped to create.

George W H Jackson

Thornbury, South Gloucestershire

CONTENTS

1. THE FAMILY HOLIDAY
2. PEMBROKESHIRE DISCOVERY
3. TIME TO MOVE
4. THE MAN WHO WOULDN'T TAKE NO FOR AN ANSWER
5. WHAT TO DO IN WINTER
6. POUNDING THE BEAT
7. DALE DAYS
8. MILFORD DAYS
9. MR. FIXIT
10. HAPPY CHRISTMAS
11. THE LAST STRAW
12. WITH THE HERALD BARD
13. PUB LANDLORD
14. SETTLING IN
15. A NEW PAINT JOB
16. MISTER TOWN CLERK
17. MEANWHILE, BACK AT THE BROOK
18. SAILORS AND SHOWMEN
19. A FEW MORE ROUNDS
20. FIRE AND SNOW
21. TIME TO CALL TIME

1: *THE FAMILY HOLIDAY*

My mother discovered Pembrokeshire in 1966. I suppose that in fairness I should say that a few Celts, Vikings and Normans beat her to it but as far as our family is concerned, Mum was definitely responsible for a discovery that was to literally change most of our lives.

Family Summer holidays had long been a tradition with us starting back in the 1930's when, before my mother and father were married, they joined up with my mother's mother and my mother's aunts and uncles to holiday in places within reasonable distance of their Bedfordshire homes such as Yarmouth and Hemsby. Adolph Hitler put a stop to this pleasure for a while but the practice resumed as soon as possible.

The very first holiday I was taken on was very soon after the end of the war in 1946 when my sister Jennifer was just a baby. It was to Bournemouth and I can clearly remember parts of the beach being fenced off because land mines were still planted and that on the parts of the beach that we were allowed to use there were still huge steel and concrete structures just off shore to obstruct the landing of any invasion fleet. As would become the norm, we were accompanied by my maternal grandmother, Gran Maud, her sister Gert and Gert's husband George Germaine – universally known as Joe as there were far too many Georges already in the family.

Another early holiday was at Polegate, near Eastbourne, where we stayed at a boarding house run by the relatives of someone the family knew. Food was still on ration and obviously in short supply because we took our own hens eggs (we kept chickens at home) to ensure that at least Jennifer had one each day for her breakfast. I remember Aunty Gert and Uncle Joe having to go up endless flights of stairs to get to their bedroom in the attic, everyone counting eggs to make sure that we got back all that we had delivered and Gert complaining most of the day when her breakfast one morning consisted of just half a kipper.

Bournemouth 1946: l to r Aunt Gert, Uncle Joe, Gran Maud, Mum and Me, Dad holding Jennifer

Over the years, the family grew with the addition of my sister Margaret and my brother Nigel and other holidays were at Jaywick Sands, near Clacton, at Hemsby north of Great Yarmouth, at Winchelsea, East Sussex and a number at Seaview on the Isle of Wight. The Hemsby holiday where we rented one or possibly two 'chalets' (wooden sheds) with no mains sewage brought back memories for Mum and Dad. Back in the 1930's there had been an outside chemical toilet into which they had been advised to 'sprinkle a little sand' after each use – not difficult as the floor consisted entirely of sand. The toilets were emptied weekly by council workmen into a tanker looking like a boat on wheels. Gran Maud in particular had been just a bit heavy-handed with the sand and what one of the men said as he staggered towards the 'boat' with his overweight load became a family catchphrase - ' Sand, sand, I'll give the buggers sand.'

On the Isle of Wight, 'Grampy' Maddocks spent the Summer in a wooden shed and rented his house to the likes of us leaving his cat behind for us to feed. He did call in most days bringing food for the cat and checking that his moggy (and no doubt his house) were still OK. One day when we headed for the beach, Gran Maud decided to stay in and enjoy a peaceful bath. When we got back, there was no sign of her but eventually feeble cries were heard from the bathroom. At first it was just the females who went to check and found that she had got in to the narrow 'wrong' end of the bath and not being a lightweight lady, was firmly stuck in water that was by now freezing cold. They failed to move her, mainly because they were helpless with laughter and as a last resort summoned the male members of the household to assist. Uncle Joe told us all to wait a minute, which we did somewhat mystified until he came back and we all fell about laughing when we saw that he had picked up a garden spade to help with the task ahead. The spade wasn't actually needed and Maud was eventually hauled out but nobody had thought to give her a towel and all she had to attempt to cover her modesty were two small flannels as the audience that included all the younger generation watched and joined in the fun.

For a number of years our holiday was in North Wales at Porth Dinllaen and then later at nearby Morfa Nefyn on the Lleyn Peninsular. Originally we rented a house literally on the beach.

We travelled by train and this involved tin trunks full of bedding and clothing being sent on days ahead by PLA (passenger luggage in advance) in the hope that it would all be there when we eventually arrived. The house was owned by a character called Mary Thomas who had a dog which she was forever cursing in Welsh. We thought for a couple of years that the dog's name was Diawl but discovered eventually that diawl meant 'little devil' normally more colloquially translated as 'bugger'. One year, Mary told us that she had re-decorated and sure enough she had – lovely new floral paper hung everywhere including over the top of pictures that she couldn't be bothered to take off the wall before getting busy with the pasting brush..

In the Summer of 1965, the family – Mum, Dad, Gran Maud, Uncle Joe (Aunt Gert had by then died), sister Jennifer with husband Paul and first child Maxine, sister Margaret, brother Nigel and me with wife Haidee and our first child Bill set off on a holiday to Winchelsea. We divided the costs by ten – the two babies went free and the total added up to £106.13s.06p.That worked out at just £10.67 each in decimal currency for a fortnight's holiday but at this time I was only earning £13.58 a week before tax.

It was always Mum who organised the family holiday. Correction – it was always Mum who organised everything. Dad was only too happy to bring his wage packet home, accept his 'pocket money' and leave Mum to do everything else. Dad was a toolmaker – skilled enough to be classified as 'reserved occupation' – too important to be called up for service in the armed forces during the war. He didn't however earn vast amounts and I am amazed looking back as to how Mum managed to bring up four children, always well fed and clothed, pay a mortgage, run a three bedroomed detached house and still save enough from that one wage for the holiday we always had

Winchelsea 1965 with sister Maggie and brother Nigel. Why the hell was I wearing a tie on holiday ?

2: PEMBROKESHIRE DISCOVERY

As with finances, the choice of venue for any holiday was again very much in Mum's hands. She would read magazines, listen to ideas and experiences from friends and when possibilities were firm in her mind she would, in those pre-internet days, spend lengthy periods researching *Dalton's Weekly,* maps and *Bradshaw's* railway timetables for places to stay and ways of getting there. Once this was done, there would be a series of letters and phone calls until she could finally announce, 'It's booked'. The result for Summer 1966 was Pembrokeshire and the village of Marloes. But I didn't go – time for a bit of background.

My parents lived in Houghton Regis, Bedfordshire where my mother had been born. Dad was from Birmingham and arrived when his factory re-located to Dunstable. He subsequently found lodgings with my grandmother, met Mum and the rest, as they say, is history. They married in 1939 and had a house built on the outskirts of the village and I was born there in 1941. I left Dunstable Grammar School aged sixteen and became a Scientific Assistant at the Meteorological Office whose headquarters were at that time in Dunstable. It was here that I met Haidee who would become my wife. I worked in four different departments at the Met Office HQ including being very much involved with their first ever computer *Meteor* and also worked operationally at RAF Bovingdon in Hertfordshire. The Met Office moved its headquarters to Bracknell in Berkshire during 1961 and it was while we were there that I married Haidee in 1962 and our first son Bill was born in 1963.

On April Fools Day 1964, having decided a career change was due (start of a pattern!), I had joined Huntingdonshire Constabulary as a Police Constable. I served my first two years or so in Huntingdon itself before being posted to the market town of St Ives. Not too long after that move our second son Douglas was born – on my 25th birthday in May 1966 and when he was less than a month old we took a holiday in Bournemouth staying for a week at the Cotford Hall Hotel.

Wedding Day 9th June 1962

Obviously we were feeling rich with the £22 Maternity Grant and the eight shillings (40p) a week Family Allowance that we became entitled to with a second child.

New recruit at training school

So, we missed out on the first ever family trip to Pembrokeshire but we very soon heard so much about it and what we heard was all good. The family had rented East Hook Farmhouse from its normal occupants Mr & Mrs Bobby Morgan. East Hook is beyond Marloes village towards Martin's Haven and my grandmother described the journey as being like driving to the edge of the World. Everyone in the family agreed (an unusual event) that Pembrokeshire was a wonderful, beautiful place and so it was that we would all holiday at East Hook for the next four Summers. By the last of these our numbers had grown to such an extent that at East Hook we occupied the farmhouse, a caravan and the first floor of a barn. The females and younger children were in the house and caravan while all the males slept on camp beds in the barn which was immediately christened 'The Monastery'

On the first of these holidays a seed was perhaps sown when unloading at Marloes Sands car park we saw a policeman (I now know to have been PC Roger Thomas) come through on his motorcycle. Gran Maud said to me, 'How would you like his job boy?' and I just smiled. How could I possible have known that one day I would literally have his job and be patrolling that same beat and even more unbelievably that later my sister

East Hook Farm, Marloes

Jennifer would divorce and move to Pembrokeshire with her, by then, six children, that then my parents would move to Pembrokeshire on their retirement and that my brother would decide to come with them.

Lovely though Pembrokeshire and its people were, we found one thing rather strange and that was the residents of Marloes often referring to residents of Dale as Frogs and people from St Ishmaels as Mice. Then we discovered Marloes people were Gulls, Haverfordwest were Longnecks and Milford people Scalybacks. Later we found that these names were somewhat formalised as St Ishmaels School had a mouse on its badge, Dale Yacht Club had a frog on its burgee and Tish Cricket Club were called The Mice in the local press. What we never discovered was why, so while writing this I did some research. This revealed more nicknames – Fishguard Herrings, Tenby Sharks, Penally Crows and St Brides Cruddlings (whatever they may be). The best suggestion for derivations came from Tom Bennett, a member of the *Pembrokeshire – I Love It Facebook* group:- Frogs because Dale people were amphibious and many frogs were found in the field below Dale Castle. St Ishmaels exported grain so mice and voles would be prevalent and Marloes people were beachcombers and scavengers just like gulls. But the origins, the when and the why remain a mystery.

In January 1968, we moved to the village of Sawtry, just off the A1 dual carriageway between Huntingdon & Peterborough into a nice detached police house within sight of the A1. The house was less than five years old and for the first time in our married life we were now 'on the phone'. People could contact us and although we would have to pay for private calls there would be no more going down the road to a phone box to call friends and family. For a long time I had envied the lifestyle of the village beat men and the way that, in many ways they were their own bosses. I had now achieved this and I knew that I would have a young Section Sergeant who, provided you did the job, was happy to let you do it your way. When, before the move, we called at our new home to measure up for curtains, etc. the current incumbent was out and his wife showed us round. I was somewhat surprised that she seemed to have no idea as to the boundaries of her husband's beat. When we moved in there was a swine fever epidemic around and within a month of our arrival, Haidee knew every village and hamlet on my 'patch' and had become expert at issuing Pig Movement Licences on my behalf to farmers calling at my office when I was out on patrol.

There was a £30 Removal Allowance over and above the cost of the removal van and after new curtains, etc. had been paid for there was a bit left over and we decided that we could afford to get a dog – for the children's benefit of course. As luck would have it some black & white Border Collie sheep dog pups were available from a farm in Glatton another village in my beat area. There had been three in the litter and they had been given the provisional names of Pip, Squeak & Wilfred. A local farmer, Joe Speechley had first choice, had already taken Pip and with great originality had re-christened him Rover. Of the other two, one looked particularly cute and friendly and we thought he would be good with the boys. We had chosen Wilfred – a stupid name for a dog but he looked very much like a Wilfred and that's what we continued to call him. So now we had another passenger for our Pembrokeshire journeys.

All three pups had started to run with their mother when she was on the farm working with animals and Joe had chosen Rover nee Pip as a working dog. He had a longer coat than the other two and looked the part but he turned out to be pretty much useless. Joe actually knocked at my door one day and asked if I would swap but Wilfred was very much part of the family by then so we refused. Years later, when we were actually living in Pembrokeshire, some cattle got into the gardens of houses next to us from the woods above and sent the holidaymaker occupants into a panic. I sent Wilfred in with the highly technical command, 'Get them out' and he rounded them up and worked them back through the gap in the fence as if he had been doing it every day of his life. The townie holidaymakers were well impressed and asked however I had managed to train him to do such a complicated job; 'Oh, it takes years' was my smug and totally untruthful reply. Wilfred's mum had obviously taught him well and Joe Speechley definitely picked the wrong dog.

I had a wife, two boys, a dog, my own patch to police, an *LE Velocette* 'Noddy' motorbike to patrol it and that would soon be replaced by a brand new G registration *Mk 1 Ford Escort* panda car – Life was good.

3: *TIME TO MOVE*

As a family we came to really like Pembrokeshire and the locals seemed to take to us. They were used then to their holidaymakers being mostly walkers or birdwatchers and it was a change for them to see a whole gang arrive in a tatty old van, have considerably more than just two halves of shandy in the pub and actually talk to them and treat them as equals. The Lobster Pot in Marloes became our regular holiday local with occasional trips to The Griffin at Dale and ventures out to the Copper Coins Club at St Ishmaels, directions to which were given to Mum by Lobster Pot regulars on her first visit in 1966 when the family set out looking for a village called 'Sunny Smiles'. Billy Rees was the landlord at the Pot and Morris Allen was running the Copper Coins at that time. We mixed in well, chatted and played darts with a group of mostly young lads in the Pot and over the years began to count them as friends. It was nevertheless a bit of a shock when one day two of them, Dai Howells and Pete Sturley, turned up at Sawtry 'just to say hello' after a journey of around 300 miles.

Billy Rees was quite a character and it was he who had applied in 1962 for a licence for the house that was to become the Lobster Pot to give Marloes its first pub in living memory despite objections from the then landlord of the Griffin at Dale. On one holiday we were joined (uninvited) by my wife's younger brother Ron who, despite his relative youth, already had a reputation for being reluctant to put his hand in his pocket. He was invariably the last to buy a round and one night when it was his turn and the rest of us stood at the bar with empty glasses (he still had an inch or so at the bottom of his) he decided to visit the gents.

With no prompting whatsoever, Billy immediately filled our glasses while brother-in-law was away and on his return said, 'knew you had forgotten to order a round. Did you want one yourself or will you make that last?'

The tatty vans that we normally arrived in, always *Bedford CA* models, were bought just for the holiday and then sold or scrapped immediately afterwards. It was in 1967 I think that one van and one car accommodated Mum and Dad, Margaret and Nigel, Jennifer and husband Paul Rayner with daughters Maxine, Helen and Paula, Gran Maud, Uncle Joe Germaine and me and Haidee with Bill and Douglas not forgetting Wilfred the dog. No wonder people in Marloes remembered us!

A Bedford CA Van of the era.

Wilfred was not too bad on the road unless it was wet and we drove through puddles, then he would start jumping about. We got some sedative from the vet and one year Haidee gave him a second dose because there were a lot of puddles around and spent the rest of the trip checking to see that he was still alive as he was completely 'zonked'. There was very little dual carriageway then and with a top speed of fifty going down hill with a following wind we would trundle down the A40, lucky to average 30mph and take all day to make the trip.

One year the van didn't quite make it, we got as far as somewhere around Llandeilo, getting slower and slower until the engine died and we discovered the rocker arms and tappets inside the rocker box totally unconnected to anything else. We got a tow to a garage, which arranged for a minibus to take us the rest of the way. The van was fixed and we collected it later in the holiday and eventually sold it at a profit, almost covering the repair costs. Another van made it back home - just! We had only got as far as Carmarthen when I noticed the steering was loose and wandering on the corners but I soldiered on with the steering getting worse and worse until after many more hours I turned it in through the gates of Mum & Dad's house. We got underneath and had a look the following day and gulped a bit when we saw that a plate in the steering mechanism with six retaining bolts had just one of those bolts left – and that was loose. That van got parked in the orchard and stayed there to rust away.

The vans were always good sport and unloading Gran Maud could be interesting with her bags and walking stick and the Wellington boots she would wear to do down the path to Marloes Sands as they 'gave her better grip'. One van in particular had worn door catches and whenever we went up anything like a steep hill, the front seat passenger and sometimes the driver too would have to hang on to the sliding doors to prevent them sliding fully open. This was a full time job going into and out of Little Haven.

One year Paul's car got a puncture that fortunately became apparent while we were still parked up at East Hook. He tried jacking the car up but the jack went straight through the bodywork that was more rust than steel. In the end, Bobby Morgan, who was built like a gypsies' greyhound, stuck a large length of timber under the car, which was a heavy old *Morris Oxford* or *Austin Cambridge* and all on his own held it up in the air while we banged the spare on. This was great – Paul had wheels but the lift had had badly twisted the rotted body and as I followed it in the van for the rest of the holiday it seemed to move like a crab and from directly behind all four wheels were visible in a row!

During those holidays, although we had travelled a long way from home, we didn't venture far from Marloes once we had arrived in Pembrokeshire and why would you? With young children wanting beaches we had Marloes Sands, St Brides, Dale, Little Haven and Broad Haven nearby. There would be probably one visit to Haverfordwest to pick up groceries and supplies. For exploring and great views there was Martins Haven and the Deer Park. For a drink there was the Lobster Pot, the Griffin and the Copper Coins. Why leave paradise? Apparently the Deer Park was created by the Kensington Estate, St Brides but they never did get round to actually keeping any deer.. It was probably my favourite place sitting on lovely soft grass watching the sea, looking at Skomer and enjoying the fact that I hadn't got sand in every orifice.

Gran Maud in her beachwear wellies

So, we liked Pembrokeshire, liked the people and some of themat least seemed to like us but there were other factors that began to take us in the direction of perhaps thinking of moving there. In January 1970, having previously passed my Sergeants promotion examination, I went on to pass the Inspector level exam and this permitted me to apply to go to the Police College at Bramshill. If you were selected as a 'Bramshill Boy' you were immediately promoted to Sergeant on graduation and to Inspector a year later with accelerated promotion through the ranks to follow. Geoff Dear, who was then my Chief Inspector, had been to Bramshill. He went on and upwards becomie Assistant Commissioner Metropolitan Police, Chief Constable of the West Midlands force, one of Her Majesty's Inspectors of Constabulary and eventually Baron Dear and Deputy Speaker of the House of Lords. He was a lovely man and once asked me to organise a tug-of-war team because I had had previous experience as part of a team that became Air Ministry Champions. I said I would if he would be anchorman – not thinking for one minute that he would agree – but he did, was very much one of the boys and smiled quite happily when I shouted at him in training for not holding the rope in the right way.

Four of us were chosen to attend a day-long selection board at Headquarters at Brampton and one was a young PC who was stationed two village beats up the A1 from me at Alwalton and had spent much of the time he had been there ringing me up to ask how to do things. The members of the board were the Deputy Chief Constable, another senior officer and Inspector Popplewell who had recently come to us as Divisional Traffic Inspector. I thought the board had gone pretty well but I didn't get the one place going. I asked Mr Popplewell some weeks later why I had not succeeded and he told me that there was nothing in it, he had voted for me but the others had thought I was 'too old'. Too old at twenty-eight! And of course it was the lad up the road who was always asking my advice who got the place. Inspector Popplewell went on to become Assistant Chief Constable of Avon & Somerset Police.

Another factor was that the way we policed rural Huntingdonshire had been 're-organised and modernised' – in other words buggered up. The Yaxley Section disappeared and

Sawtry became one of four rural beats in the Ramsey 'Sector' (a fancy new name for a Sub-Division). We were supposed to fit enquiries and incidents into 'fixed route' patrols that were designed to do nothing but remove initiative, make things more complicated and save petrol. 'My' car was taken away on my rest days and sometimes when I was working to become a 'Sector Mobile' driven by one of the Ramsey men.

The theory was that the Sector Mobile would cover our areas when we were off duty but in practice all it meant was that we were unable to respond to minor happenings in the village that we would have normally done even though we were technically off duty and that 'the townies' in the Sector Mobiles came in and trampled all over relationships we had taken a long time to cultivate. Increasingly I was also called in to cover shifts in the town of Ramsey itself and this again meant less and less time doing 'proper' rural policing. As far as the 'fixed routes' were concerned I soon started to basically ignore them and do my own thing. If you were discovered 'off route' there was always an excuse – a driver had flagged you down to report stray cows on the road, etc. So if HQ asked for my location I always told them where I actually was rather than where I was supposed to be, unlike a colleague who gave his location as A1 Norman Cross when he was actually five miles away only to have HQ come back with, 'Then no doubt you can see the seven vehicle accident at that location'.

We had also been looking at the possibility of buying our own house as this was now permitted and a fairly reasonable Rent Allowance was paid that would have helped with the mortgage but around the Huntingdon area at that time anything bigger than a rabbit hutch and with more than a pocket handkerchief sized garden was beyond our limits. Property in Pembrokeshire was then considerably cheaper. Our holiday that year was again to Marloes and when we saw a house for sale in nearby Dale at a very sensible price we were tempted. More than tempted in fact because no matter that I hadn't applied for a transfer, no matter that jobs were in short supply in Pembrokeshire and no matter that we hadn't got money for the deposit, we offered £3,750 and it was accepted.

That year, 1969-70 my gross pay was £1095. It had finally started to go up after a long time under Harold Wilson as Labour Prime Minister when our pay virtually stood still and I had now passed the magic £1,000 that I thought when I started at the Met Office would make me really well off. It didn't make me rich but I don't suppose it was too bad as Dad was only on £25.67 a week at that time – not that much more. The deposit was covered by a loan of £300 from a great uncle but then there was a major hiccup when Abbey National decided to withhold £300 of the mortgage advance until we had replaced all the windows, which were steel and very corroded by the salt air. This time it was the vendor who came to the rescue. Dr Butler owned both halves of the semi-detached pair as holiday homes, was selling one and retaining the other and to keep the sale alive he agreed a second mortgage of £300 at 10% over three years. I well remember having to sit down and write him thirty-six post dated cheques and being in the strange position of making mortgage payments to our next-door neighbour. So we became the proud owners of 77 Blue Anchor Way, Dale.

Not long before we left St Ives a fairly elderly Detective Constable called Norman Pipe had moved in next door. He was one of the boys, always good for a laugh and didn't seem to mind that he had been passed over as far as promotion was concerned. After I had moved to Sawtry and when the very senior officer he had upset years before eventually retired he was soon promoted to Sergeant and then even more quickly to

Inspector. When he was posted in as one of my Section Inspectors I was amazed to find that he had become a real bastard, a pig of a man and he seemed to save his best porcine impressions for me apparently because I had known him when he was taking the piss out of Inspectors rather than trying and failing to be one. We ended up hating each other's guts. He would get at me by sending back perfectly good reports three or four times, generally hounding me and following me round trying to catch me at something I shouldn't have been doing. I responded with insolent politeness and by going as far as I could without him actually being able to report me.

Wilfred enjoys Marloes Sands

Haidee enjoys Broad Haven

One night at Sawtry I was due to go off duty at 10pm and as I drove along the A1 I saw his car parked up near my house no doubt with the hope of catching me going off duty early. I carried on past my turning, went into the village by a different road and at about five to ten I radioed Headquarters to say that I was going off-watch on foot patrol. There were no pocket radios in those days and once I left the car I couldn't be contacted. I parked the car in a prominent spot in the centre of the village near The Green and strolled off to spend an hour in the warmth and comfort of the back room at The Chequers. I finally got back home around eleven to find my Inspector 'friend' freezing cold and hovering about six inches off the ground in anger. He knew that I had done it on purpose but how can you report a man who has given up an hour of his own time to go on foot patrol on a cold night to look for a persistent coal thief and had followed all correct radio procedures to the letter so that everyone (except the Inspector) knew what he was doing?

It was a police ritual that whenever you were 'met' on patrol by a Sergeant or Officer, they would prove that they were doing their job by signing your notebook. A lot didn't always bother but of course Pipe always insisted. Because of this and just to annoy him, I would always ensure that my book was bang up to date and shove it under his nose for signature before he had chance to ask for it. Then I would remind him that under the relevant Force Order I should strictly speaking also sign his book. If his wasn't up to date I could tut-tut and ask him how much space he would like me to leave. This all came in handy later when during one of our rows he threatened to report me for insubordination and I was able to point out that all the signatures in my book would be proof enough to report him for 'oppressive or tyrannical conduct towards an inferior in rank'. Basically it was all about him not being up to the job, me being capable of doing his job standing on my head and him knowing it. Long before all this happened I had decided to apply for a transfer to Wales. He wasn't the cause of me going but he certainly helped to confirm that I had made the right move – the bastard.

4. THE MAN WHO WOULDN'T TAKE NO FOR AN ANSWER

I started applying for jobs in Pembrokeshire without success and then applied to Dyfed Powys Police for a transfer. On 17 September 1970 I received the reply that, as I had purchased a house in Dale, I couldn't say that I would be willing to work anywhere within the Dyfed Powys area and therefore my request was refused.

We took possession of 77 Blue Anchor Way in February 1971 and I went down on my own and literally camped out in the house to do a bit of clearing up and gardening and to arrange for the windows to be replaced. Stewart Fisher from Jubilee Villas and Harry Llewellyn took on the job and it cost us £207.09 to replace the lot with similar metal-framed windows (yes, we had gone decimal by the time I got the bill). The weather was fabulous and I remember being out in the garden at number 77 in shirtsleeves and feeling very warm.

On 27 February I wrote again to Dyfed Powys Police and said I was moving to Dale no matter what, that this was their last chance to acquire a good copper (or words to that effect) and applied again for a transfer. To my surprise a reply came back inviting me to an interview on Monday 15 March. I went down the night before and spent a miserable night in the only hotel in Carmarthen that had a vacancy. It wasn't that all the other hotels were full but Carmarthenshire was still 'dry' on Sundays and people used to 'book into' hotels so that as 'residents' they could get a drink. My hotel was the Temperance Hotel – no drink and a church clock about ten yards from my bedroom window that chimed every bloody hour.

The following day at the appointed hour I was amazed to be ushered into the presence of Chief Constable himself - J R Jones, or John Ron as I later got to call him. This would normally have been unheard of for just a job interview. He sat me down, then stood up and started walking in circles around my chair. At last he spoke and totally took me by surprise with, 'So this is him. At last I get to see what he looks like. This is him, the Great Jackson, the man who won't take no for an answer'. He then said, 'Are you willing to serve anywhere in my force area?' Although I'd just bought my house, I gave the answer I knew he wanted, 'Yes' and that was about it, all that was left was to sort out an effective date of transfer and for him to tell my Chief Constable that he was taking me.

What had happened was that he had decided to close a number of village stations including PC Roger Thomas's at Mullock, which covered Marloes, Dale, St Ishmaels, part of Little Haven and a few hamlets in between. There had been an outcry from local residents and Parish Councils and with me moving into Dale he was now able to save the situation by saying that they could retain a village bobby during the summer months and save face by saying that I would have to work in Milford Haven during the winter months when there were no tourists. He was happy, the locals were happy and we were more than happy.

The next few weeks passed in a flash, we booked the wonderfully named *T for Transport* to move us to Dale over 21 and 22 April 1971 at a cost of £85 and said goodbye to 74 Fen Lane, Sawtry. In an ironic twist, we had never had central heating in any of our police houses and just before we left we had all the dust and inconvenience of having it installed without ever getting the pleasure of using it. We stayed overnight at Wrestlingworth with Haidee's Mother and then set off to follow our furniture but we only got as far as Shefford before the clutch went on the *Hillman Imp*. Leaving the car there, we hired a *Triumph Toledo* and finally caught up with our furniture only a few miles outside Dale. Not the best of starts - £24.64 for a new clutch, £10.00 for four days car hire plus £13.48 for excess mileage and petrol charged and another trip backwards and forwards to return the *Toledo* and collect the repaired *Imp*. The 25 April was my effective transfer date and the following day I was sworn in at Haverfordwest Magistrates Court and collected my new uniform. I was now PC149

The next big job was to collect my transport. I was quite pleased to find that I was back on two wheels, not so pleased to discover that the two wheels belonged to a 250cc *BSA Fleetstar*, probably the last and without doubt the worst model ever made by *BSA* and that I wasn't even being given any proper motorcycle clothing to ride it – just a normal Mac and a very poor crash helmet. Like the swearing in, where I never stopped being a policeman but I still had to be sworn in again, I never stopped being qualified to ride police motorcycles but I still had to take another test. I met an elderly traffic PC on a big bike at Haverfordwest. He followed me to Dale, sent me home while he carried on to see Joe Griffiths who was the Coastguard chief in the village and a friend of his, stayed there for tea and a chat and then nearly an hour later, came back to my house to tell me that I'd passed!

The clothing situation was solved fairly quickly (for Wales) and it wasn't too long before I had bullied them into giving me a proper bike suit and later a decent 'pilot' crash helmet with a good fitted visor. All I needed then was a pair of 'Elvis Presley' chrome plated sunglasses and I was off to explore and pose around my new beat. Most of the locals seemed genuinely pleased to see me and to have 'their' policeman again and because of our holidays in the area I already knew a fair number of people. The weather was good and this suited me well as second time round on motorbikes I was older and wiser and very much a fair weather rider.

We had to keep a daily log of routes and mileage and on a fine day I would clock up plenty of miles for the wet days when most of my patrols would be done on paper. Keeping in radio contact from my armchair was a slight problem but I soon discovered that riding at a certain speed over a certain stretch of bumpy road was guaranteed to put the radio out of action and the supply of spares was very limited. Once my radio was u/s, Haidee would take telephone messages and having given them careful consideration I would decide if and when to 'come back off patrol' and respond to them. I didn't always need to resort to such underhand practices though as the *Fleetstar* was so unreliable that I normally had one under repair, one waiting for spares and one on the road if I was lucky (or unlucky according to the weather). A spare car or mini-van would sometimes be available but either way I didn't often get wet.

Being back on a motorbike brought the usual quota of embarrassing moments. I had stopped a motorist to give him a rollicking for a particularly dodgy bit of driving. I did a quick check of his car after the initial browbeating and finding nothing really wrong, I gave him a stern lecture on the fact that his tyres were very close to the legal tread depth limit and the need for regular checks on their condition. Having done my 'bastard' bit for the day, I climbed back on my bike and roared away only to have the back tyre blow out about fifty yards up the road. To his credit he didn't actually laugh out loud as he drove past leaving me in the wilds of Talbenny to push the bike nearly a mile to the nearest farm.

On a Fleetstar Leading Milford Carnival 1971

On another occasion I had cautioned a young biker for having a faulty exhaust and gave him a long lecture about how tampering with the silencer, apart from being illegal, would probably ruin his engine in the long run. I didn't have a long run because this time I had gone no more than twenty yards before my engine blew up in a cloud of blue smoke. Fortunately I was on the sea front at Dale so my walk was a lot shorter this time.

I only ever parted company with the bike once. I was on my way back home to Dale on a very dark and wet night and was totally soaked having ploughed through a very deep unseen puddle between Slatemilll Bridge and Mullock. (Only in Pembrokeshire

Riding one of the dire Fleetstar 250cc fleet

can water gather at the TOP of a hill). I crossed Mullock Bridge and was on my way up the hill towards Crabhall Farm when there was a loud bang, my front wheel came off the ground and I was thrown off onto the roadside bank. There was very little damage to me or the bike with both suffering just cuts and bruises but me with the added injury of having to submit an accident report and being even wetter. I discovered that I had hit a large stone which had apparently fallen from the bank but could see no obvious place where it had come from. I discovered later that the stone had been put on top of the bank to secure a hand-written direction sign to Philbeach Farm where a delivery had been expected. The sign had been removed but not the stone and I hope that the gentleman responsible had a few troubled days awaiting my knock at the door. I didn't bother.

Mention of Talbenny and of sunglasses brings back memories of the Pembrokeshire Motor Club meetings held at the old Talbenny airfield which were probably at their peak from the mid 1970s to the early 1980s. During this period it was the venue for rounds of both the British Sprint Championship and the British Rally Cross Championship putting it up in the same league as the likes of Duxford, Lydden Hill, Thruxton, Knock Hill and Goodwood. We became quite fans and often attended throughout the year to watch converted saloon cars, specials and proper racing cars like *Mallock, Lotus* and *March* doing their thing over the short course. I first discovered the sport when I attended on duty (it was on my patch!) just to have a look. Obviously an occasion for posing on the motor bike with the 'Elvis' sunglasses and spending plenty of time soaking it all in. Unfortunately I also soaked in a fairly strong sun and a more than gentle breeze leaving me with a lovely pair of white 'panda' eyes for several days afterwards. The public address commentary at Talbenny was frequently done by Richard Davies of Richard Davies Tyres in Haverfordwest and years later after we had left Pembrokeshire and were making the first of many visits to the Castle Combe circuit in Wiltshire, it was a really pleasant surprise to hear his voice over the loudspeakers again.

We were made very welcome as new residents in Dale with one notable exception. As a new local policeman and a new parishioner, I had expected a visit or contact at least from the local Vicar who lived in the village but nothing was forthcoming. I soon discovered that he had been disqualified from driving after failing a breath test but that shouldn't have been a problem for him as the vicarage was only a very short walk away. Months later, very soon after he got his licence back, Rev. C.D.Lynn Griffiths eventually came knocking on our door having got over his apparent sulk and wondering why he hadn't seen us in church. I told him that I only got one Sunday off every month and didn't like to waste it. Before too long Rev. Griffiths moved on and his replacement was much more human, joining the Coronation Hall committee and enjoying a pint of *Guinness* in the Griffin afterwards.

We knew that we had been totally accepted when we were asked if we were interested in potato picking and with cash somewhat tight we were happy to say yes. Strictly speaking, police regulations did not permit any other employment at that time but I had established that there was a very relaxed attitude towards anything agricultural. We had been asked by Clem Warlow who lived in Blue Anchor Way but farmed with his sons at Broomhill Farm, St Anns Head and was one of the many in those days who grew Pembrokeshire Earlies all of which were picked by hand and were absolutely delicious.

A tractor would 'spin out' a row which would be divided into 'pitches' for picking, sometimes double pitches for pickers working as a pair. Every potato spun out was carefully but quickly picked up into a small container and then transferred to the picker's paper bag with a capacity of 56lbs (approx 25Kg). Once the row was cleared, the tractor would spin out another and the process was pretty much continuous and back-breaking. As soon as pickers had filled their first bag, weighing would begin and this was where I was lucky. The great majority of pickers were female so in the best sexist tradition, as a man I would at this point be withdrawn from picking to become a weigher. Weighers normally worked in pairs going from pitch to pitch with a set of balance scales and a 56lb weight juggling potatoes between the bag being weighed and the picker's next bag until it was spot on. As soon as we were happy with the weight the bag would be sealed with a metal tie. Weighed bags were tallied and taken to a central point where at the end of the day, my job would then be to hump the bags onto an elevator for them to be loaded aboard a lorry for transport away.

Payment was always cash in hand plus a 'feed' of potatoes. Clem and his sons were always generous and the 'feed' would normally be several pounds to which you helped yourself and very few were too greedy. Other farmers were less generous and Megan Brian at Dale Hill Farm used to physically weigh out a much smaller amount. After the first day of picking you struggled to walk upright but it got better as you got used to it and if you have never tasted Pembrokeshire spuds straight from the field after a hard day's picking, you haven't lived. The other benefit for me was the banter with the mainly female band of pickers. We all got to know each other very quickly and being able to demonstrate that their new copper was actually quite human was a big part of fitting in.

I still enjoyed a pint or so, which was just as well because in rural areas a lot of work centred on pubs. They were often the centre of the community and an hour spent in a bar was often more productive than eight hours on patrol or pounding the beat. With a couple of drinks to relax them people would report incidents and crimes and pass on information and gossip that they would never have thought of doing if they had needed to stop you in the street or call at your home. In the opposite direction quiet warnings could be administered and you could let it be known that you knew that certain things were going on secure in the knowledge that it would get back to those concerned quicker than any telegram. Criminals used pubs, informants used pubs and we used pubs and one of the most important skills was knowing which people used which pubs at which time and which landlords served free beer when police business was slack. On my Dale beat I had plenty to choose from. When I first arrived there was The Griffin at Dale (Bill and Paddy Tamsett), The Lobster Pot at Marloes (Dennis and June Blackman), The Brook at St Ishmaels (Malcolm Rowlands), The Taberna Inn at Herbrandston (Reg & Billy Mathias), The Welcome Traveller at Tiers Cross (John Twigg), The Swan Inn at Littlehaven (Cliff Wilkinson), The St Brides Hotel at Little Haven (Eric Bradley), The Little Haven Hotel (K Marsden), The Copper Coins Club at St Ishmaels (Frank Dunn), The St Ishmaels Sports and Social Club, The Hasguard Cross Social Club (Billy Thomas) and of course Dale Yacht Club. All these were on my patch so I was never too restricted in choice.

I always tried to spend the last hour or so of every evening shift in one of these pubs and I felt quite cheated if an incident kept me tied up until after closing time. I never went out after nine-o-clock without a civvy jacket on the back seat of my patrol car and if I was lumbered with a motorbike I would either switch to my own car for the last patrol or choose a pub within walking distance and leave the bike at home. It was always in the landlord's interest to be friendly and most genuinely were anyway so I was always welcome in the pubs on my beat and did my best to be of some service in return. In the Lobster Pot for instance, which was well frequented by holidaymakers in season, I had an agreement with Dennis Blackman that suited us both very well. I would appear in a civvy jacket as a customer, drink for an hour or so, disappear for a few minutes just before closing time and then come back in full uniform to throw all of the holidaymakers out. This done the uniform would come off again and I would stay for a couple more drinks with the locals in the back room.

It was the Lobster Pot that very nearly caused my downfall once and that was during daylight hours! An auction was being held in the pub car park and I had gone along to control traffic, keep the crowds in order and look for a bargain (not necessarily in that order). The auction had only just got underway when June Blackman invited me in for a cup of coffee or something stronger. I avoided temptation and settled for the coffee but made the mistake of mentioning to one of the lads in the bar that it was my birthday. The immediate response was a little drop of something to warm up my coffee and from then on whether I was outside at the auction or back in the bar, I was plied with a never-ending succession of small glasses full of various fiery liquids. By three in the afternoon I had purchased spanners and screwdrivers I would probably never use, bought a brand new foot pump that fell apart the first time I used it, was two hours late for my meal break and was virtually legless.

Having just about enough sense left to realise that it wouldn't look too good if the local copper passed out in public, I decided that it was time to go home. I dropped the motorbike twice before finally managing to climb aboard and start the thing only to ride straight into the grass bank on the opposite side of the road. Fortunately the auction was over by then, the crowd were all inside the pub and if there was anyone left outside to witness my antics they were either too pissed to notice or too kind to say anything afterwards. I eventually got started again and managed to navigate the four miles back to Dale via a few grass verges but without actually falling off again. Haidee's Mother June was staying with us at the time and I don't think she was too impressed by the sight of her upright police officer son-in-law swaying through the back door surrounded by a cloud of whisky fumes, clutching a foot pump under his arm and wearing a wide grin and a uniform covered in bits of grass. I managed to pretend I was enjoying my cremated lunch and I think I had recovered enough to go out for another 'birthday drink' with the family that evening. The memory is a bit hazy but I know I didn't enjoy the second part of my birthday as much as the first.

Of course, living in Dale, my local was the Griffin and it was there that I got to know many of the residents. The pub was run by Bill and Paddy Tamsett. Paddy was very much the live wire in the pub and also took an active role in the village as a member of the Women's Institute, etc. Bill, to be kind, was rather less active. In fact some locals were cruel enough to suggest that his former service in RN Submarines meant that he had suffered from a lack of oxygen which had caused a form of permanent sleeping sickness accounting for his lack of speed behind the bar.

Among the regulars I remember is Sid Brooks who ran the petrol pumps in the village and was our milkman. Sid lacked a bit of spacial awareness and if you chatted to him while standing at the bar, you would soon find yourself a few feet further along as you unconsciously moved back to protect your personal space. George Sturley was from Marloes but often in the Griffin as he worked at Dale Sailing Company and crewed the *Dale Queen* to Skomer in the Summer. He always had a good story to tell, often complaining about the driving of holidaymakers and wondering how so many of them actually made it here alive. The Tamsetts owned one, maybe two cats of the Siamese type which much to George's (and many others) annoyance used to get up and walk on the bar close to you and your glass. George was extremely skilled at 'accidentally' bringing his lighted cigarette into the close proximity of the cat's backside causing it to leap off the bar with a yowl and then looking totally innocent when Paddy looked suspiciously at him. Unfortunately, George died in a house fire at his home some years later.

.At some time during each shift I would go into Milford Haven, which was my Sub-Divisional station to pick up and take in paper work. Nowadays it would be considered grossly over-staffed for a town with a population of around 15,000. There was a Chief Inspector (Brian Bebb) and later an Inspector as well, four Sergeants (Dai Phillips, Les Smith, Charlie Morris and Alex Jenkins), a Detective Sergeant (Kevin Owen), two Detective Constables, one WPC, around seventeen uniformed PC's, a Civilian Clerk, a Typist and one Traffic Warden. There were three other 'rural beat' officers Frank Donnelly and Monty Burton at Neyland, Terry 'Tiger' Martin at Llangwm and me half and half at Dale. Quite a few to get to know but I soon made a pretty good start. One thing that puzzled me though was that one shift was universally known as 'The Gurkhas'. After wondering for a couple of weeks and seeing no sign of funny shaped knives, curiosity got the better of me and I asked their Sergeant to explain. To which he replied, 'they're just like the bloody Gurkhas – they never take prisoners'!

In the previous paragraph I mentioned Tiger Martin. He was the village beat man at Llangwm and had a really dry sense of humour. A Breton fisherman had been arrested in Milford for being drunk and disorderly and some time later I was in the station when his skipper arrived to try to tell us that he was ready to sail and would really like his crewman back. The skipper spoke about three words of English, two of which were swear words, and we were making pretty slow progress with a combination of my rusty (failed 'O' Level) French and the Duty Sergeant's Welsh, which bore some resemblance to the Breton dialect.

Things were beginning to get a bit heated when Tiger strolled into the station. He summed up the situation instantly and turning to the Skipper said in perfect French, 'good evening captain, what can we do to help you'. We stood with our mouths open amazed at Tiger's previously hidden linguistic talent and the skipper, a great look of relief flooding his face, began to pour out a torrent of rapid French. Tiger listened with an understanding smile and when the skipper finally paused for breath said, 'Non comprend Frog mate' and casually walked off down the corridor. Tiger once put in a lengthy report asking for a garden path to be installed at his Llangwm police mansion and several weeks later was given – a rotary clothes line. Apart from defeating the whole object, a rotary clothes line doesn't keep your feet dry when you're picking lettuces in your lunch hour to sell on your beat that afternoon, it made us wonder what the hell Headquarters would have given him if he had asked for a rotary clothesline in the first place.

5: *WHAT TO DO IN WINTER ?*

The first summer in Dale had gone very well. Douglas had started school when we arrived and both he and Bill had settled in well and made friends especially Danny and Robin Copley. We were very lucky that the school was in the village with Headmaster C.A.B.Brand who was happy to take Douglas before he was actually five. Through their time at the school the boys were mainly taught by a no-nonsense man from the North of England, Stan Truelove. Stan, who became Head when Mr Brand retired, was a great teacher managing to be liked by both children and parents. I remember a Gary Glitter song (I know!) being adapted by the boys as 'I love, you love, old Stanley Truelove'. He eventually saw both the boys safely through to Milford Haven Grammar School. Haidee had been made very welcome in the village and had joined the W.I. and I was looking forward to my first season playing darts for the Lobster Pot at Marloes in the Haverfordwest League.

In that first summer, we were able to extend our Pembrokeshire horizons further. Dale beach was just a few yards away and we found and explored Watwick, West Dale and the coastal path all round the Dale peninsular. We trekked down to Lindsway Bay at St Ishmaels following in the steps of Prince Charles who had set foot on Welsh soil for the first time there in 1955 when the Royal Yacht Britannia was moored in Dale Roads. In the other direction, we discovered Newgale, Solva and St Davids. There were drives across the Preselis and discovery of the weird attraction of Porthgain. The Cleddau Bridge didn't open until March 1975 so South Pembrokeshire was still a foreign country. I was sometimes asked why I had moved to Pembrokeshire when I wasn't a beach person and never got into sailing. The answer was that I was never a particularly strong swimmer, I didn't like sand and I didn't like any pastime which involved starting out with a wet arse. But I loved looking at all those activities, the sea and the scenery and I liked the people.

The end of the summer did however pose a problem and a continuing mystery for my Chief Inspector Brian Bebb – what the hell to do with me in the winter! The Chief Constable, J R Jones, had solved his problem with the Dale and Marloes residents but hadn't given any thought as to how I would be employed during the period he had decided that they would have to be without their village bobby. There was a lot of construction work going on extending the *Esso* refinery and at the *Amoco* site with hundreds if not thousands of 'travelling men' living in on-site hostels and in lodgings around Milford so in my first winter in Milford it was decided that I would be 'Refinery Construction Site Liaison Officer'.

The idea was that I would deal with all the Summonses and Warrants that tended to follow some of the men around the country, deal with any other enquiries that required on-site attendance and start gathering criminal intelligence and other information on people and companies involved. It sounded good but all I could foresee was a lot of tramping through mud. It sort of worked but some of the lads hadn't grasped the principle of intelligence collation and treated information as personal property and others were possibly a bit jealous that while they were out in the wet and the cold, I could choose to sit in the warm playing with my very own card index system. Sergeants also soon realised that it was possible to use me to plug holes in their shifts caused by leave, sickness and courses and I tended to get used more and more in that role.

Winters remained a problem for them though and in future years I would be sent on Senior Constable's Refresher Courses, be attached for three months as a plain clothes CID Aide and be sent on a CID Course at Bristol. My 'parishioners' in Dale, Marloes and St Ishmaels also had to get used to me being taken away from them in the winter months but some never really did and I continued to get occasional telephone calls and knocks at the door reporting various things or seeking help. This was never really a problem and sometimes gave me the opportunity to go on duty in Milford Haven and then come straight back out to 'my patch' to deal with something. It also led to a lovely quote when Mrs Lloyd-Plillips of Dale Castle telephoned Milford and asked the Inspector, 'Have we got a local policeman now? I know PC Jackson is still Chairman of the Carnival Committee'.

An incident during the refinery construction period highlighted the total lack of high-level management skills or appreciation of working conditions 'at the coal face'. With so many travelling men around, Milford was a bit like a Wild West town with regular fights in a number of pubs and drunks most nights on the streets, so what did they give us as an all purpose vehicle to cope with all this action – a two-door *Austin 1100*. Unless you have ever tried to get a violent or incapable drunk into the back seat of a two-door car, you couldn't even start to imagine how ridiculous this was. One night we had a report of a drunk laying on a pavement in Hakin and I attended with Roger Inward, who was fairly small for a copper We found a very large, totally unconscious Paddy and had a hell of a job getting him into the back of the *1100*, finally realising that the reason the door wouldn't shut was that his leg was still hanging out. Having got the leg in, we then found his head was hanging out of the other side, put that in and after a similar struggle back at the nick finally got him into a cell. When he woke up in the early hours, he complained not only of a sore leg but also that we had stolen his false teeth! He was reunited with them before he was bailed but not until we had retrieved them from the gutter where they had fallen during the struggle to get him into the car.

Working in Milford, especially moving round among the four different shifts gave me a great chance to get to know everyone better. When I had first started, there were a few who didn't know quite what to make of this strange 'Saesnaeg' who had come in from abroad and had been given a country beat that had been closed with one of their own in post and then miraculously re-opened. I heard a couple of whispers on the lines of 'Look at his long hair and sideboards' and Sergeant Alex Jenkins, obviously jealous of my soft and silky pale blue Mid Anglia *Van Heusen* shirts once jokingly accused me of wearing blouses but generally I was accepted and once I had proved that I could more than do the job I became 'one of the boys' – so much so that by my second winter I had launched the *Milford Mercury* an 'underground' periodical produced in triplicate on the station typewriter with 'news' and articles gently taking the piss out of my colleagues and senior officers. After the first few editions even the Chief Inspector began to ask when the next edition would be coming out and for me to make sure that he had first read. The *Mercury* proved to be a worthy successor to my *Ramsey Record* and *St Ives Gazette* of an earlier life. The *Mercury* eventually extended to fourteen editions between December 1972 and Christmas 1975 and here are a few extracts just to give you a flavour:-

Bookings wanted for clubs, cabarets, etc. Cheerful Trev Millichip- Welsh comedian 'wide of girth and full of mirth, Tel. 2351 ext 3 (Dc later promoted Sgt.)

Join the Milford Haven Colour TV Watchers Club – Chairman Alan Coles, Sec. Arthur Howells, President Pancho Dudley. Regular meetings are held to discuss the quality of the previous night's reception and the piteous plight of those who haven't got one. (Dc later promoted Det.Sgt, Civilian Clerk & Pc)

SOS Mr Roger Inward is anxious to trace anyone who was in Broad Haven on Friday 22 December and who may be able to help him with his enquiries as to what exactly he did that night. (Pc later transferred to South Wales Police)

We offer congratulations to Miss Sue Brien on her election to the exclusive 'Ton Club' membership of which is only open to those who have caused at least £100 worth of damage to a police vehicle. On the same subject, imagine yourself in the following circumstances:- You have just driven a police vehicle right up the backside of the car in front. You are miles from home in a different Force area. You sit trembling with dread as the Traffic Sergeant dealing with the accident strides towards you with a purposeful look in his eye. He looks at you long and hard and eventually speaks saying, 'Are you married lovely?'. Must be nice being a woman. (WPc transferred to Bermuda but later returned to Milford

We extend best wishes to Mr Dennis Hughes at present away on a driving course and trust that he will learn as much about driving as the other occupants of the car will learn about North Wales, cardiography and bowls. (Pc often on Station Duty)

Flags were flown from the Police Station and the Town Hall on Monday 29th in recognition of the fact that Mary Jeffrey arrived for work at 08.58. Unfortunately the strain proved too much as she had to go off duty sick at 4pm (Civilian Typist who left to work for the same company as my brother)

It was recently noted that a certain Constable's pigeon hole was empty but closer examination showed that the bottom had collapsed under the weight. (That would be me)

There has been widespread reaction to the recent news that Ernie Jones has moved to Traffic. HQ have doubled their estimates for Alcotest tubes in the next financial year, consideration is being given to Haverfordwest Magistrates Court sitting three times a week, four disqualified drivers have decided to emigrate and work has started on a tunnel which will eventually link Blue Anchor Way, Dale with several local hostelries. (PC who transferred to Traffic Department. *Alcotest* tubes were used in the early breathalysers and I lived in Blue Anchor Way*)*

Did you know that on one Saturday night recently, Rod Evans had one Sergeant, one Inspector and one Chief Inspector with no-one else to supervise but him. They still couldn't find him despite the fact that they were all on Beat 1 (Pc with a gift for elusiveness)

Fact from the Chief Constable's Annual Report: In the Dyfed Powys Police area there is one 'full' Licensed Premises for every 341 inhabitants. No wonder it gets so bloody crowded in the Griffin. (My local in Dale)

Did you know that a certain officer given an enquiry for 74 Charles Street duly deposited it back in the tray marked 'No reply 3pm & 5pm'. So what? 74 Charles Street is Brunt's Greengrocers and it wasn't early closing day. You can't win 'em all. (I cannot remember who this was but I guarantee that everyone knew at the time)

Did you know that the wind is stronger at Milford than at Dale and that in Milford the wind can blow through walls. Did you also know that the average life of a motorcycle windscreen in Dale is four years but at Milford is ten hours? (For some reason I had had to leave my motorcycle at Milford returning to find the windscreen smashed. The damage was blamed on the wind but I knew that someone must have been messing with it)

Situation Vacant: Civilian Clerk, Milford Haven Police Station. Duties include telling someone when the telephone is ringing, finding a police officer to deal with any visitor to the enquiry desk, locking doors and turning off lights. Ability to read and write desirable but not essential. (Retirement of Arthur Howells)

Mention earlier of the travelling men reminds me of a time later when a strike at the *Esso* site got a bit interesting. Normally a handful of bored coppers stood and watched a handful of equally bored pickets with neither handful really quite sure why they were there but this one was different. As usual it took a few days to get things properly sorted out – on the first day a mass picket of at least three hundred men had no problems totally blockading the refinery while no more that six or seven policemen could only stand and watch. The second day saw coach loads of police from all over the force area watching a dozen or so pickets and on the third day we were back to being hopelessly outnumbered. It was the fourth day before we finally got it right with equal numbers on both sides and the opportunity for a bit of sport and by day five this was literally the case as a police versus pickets football match was arranged I was called in to help and on arrival I went straight to one of our vans for a sit down and a smoke. Several equally experienced colleagues were already in the van and I settled down for a yarn with some of the boys not involved in the serious game of cards taking place in a cloud of cigarette smoke at the far end of the vehicle. I had been there for about an hour when the rear door was wrenched open by a particularly useless Superintendent known to us all as Terry 'The Tit' Evans.

As the smoke cleared, he began to wonder in a very loud voice what we were all doing there but one of the lads made him stop and think (you could see the wheels turning) by saying that the Chief Superintendent had told us to keep a low profile. Not to be beaten, The Tit said, 'well there are still too many of you keeping it' and just because I happened to be nearest he told me to, 'go and stand over there'. Having received no answer to my query as to just what I was expected to do 'over there', I wandered over and just stood. I had been there no more than thirty seconds before Terry the Tit came charging over and almost screamed, 'what are you doing there in a crash helmet? You can't stand there in a crash helmet, they'll think we're expecting trouble. Go and get back in the van'. So that's just what I did and for the rest of the day I was able to counter every attempt to move me by saying, 'the Super says I'm not allowed out there in a crash helmet' until an Inspector finally got fed up and sent me home.

On the first day of this particular dispute we had been called in at short notice and in his panic the Inspector had forgotten to tell us to bring a packed lunch. This meant that he had to make arrangements for feeding us so we were sent two at a time into Milford Haven to Rabaiotti's Café in Charles Street. Two of our younger colleagues were the first to go and when they came back to relieve us, my mate and I, who were considerably longer in the tooth asked what they had had and how much had it cost. They told us that they had ordered fish and chips and that the café had said that there was nothing to pay as the food would be charged to the police station's monthly account for the supply of prisoner's meals. Having established that no signatures were required we retired to the café and ordered two huge sirloin steaks with all the trimmings. The meal was excellent and knowing that it cost about five times our usual Refreshment Allowance made it taste even better. The following day we were all restricted to sausage and chips and had to sign for it and by day three we had all received very firm instructions to bring a packed lunch but as the two of us chewed our bread and cheese we could still taste the steak and the sweetness of the success of beating the system at least once.

The strike was led as usual by a few travelling men, mostly from Glasgow but a lot of local boys were involved in the picket and we had a pretty good relationship going with them. At one time about twenty of us were trying to force a way through a very solid mass of humanity for a management car. Helmets were going astray, clothing getting torn, feet getting stamped on and tempers were beginning to fray on both sides. In the middle of all this a voice about two inches from my right ear broke off from shouting, 'fascist pigs out' to say rather more quietly, 'Hello George, see you in The Griffin tonight for a game of darts'. We were still making very little progress and our heavyweight leader Sergeant Dai Phillips was getting noticeably redder and redder in the face with the effort. Suddenly everything changed when a loud voice with a broad Pembrokeshire accent said, 'We'd better let it though now lads otherwise old Dai will have a bloody heart attack'.

When the construction work was all over and the Secretary of State for Wales came to officially open the *Amoco* refinery, I covered the event in the *Milford Mercury* thanking everyone involved as follows:-

'A certain Sergeant who, bored with the whole proceedings and unable to find where they had stored the champagne, took to the air in the Minister's helicopter and spent a happy half hour reliving past glories as a member of the RAF.

And a certain Chief Inspector who, when he found out, was hovering almost as high as the chopper because he had wanted a ride himself and the pilot had said no.

And a certain very senior CID Officer who, nose glowing as red as the Secretary of State's buttonhole, set off on a tour of the refinery jetty to see the handling of dangerously inflammable materials puffing contentedly on a huge cigar.

And a certain Inspector who, thinking the convoy of dignitaries had passed his position, headed for home and then attempted to break the world land speed record when the car containing the Chief Constable passed him in the opposite direction.

And a certain PC who, standing forlornly at the side of the Dale road said, 'I've been standing here for four hours now and I still don't know why'.

And a certain refinery security officer who, seeing the Secretary of State arrive in a high speed motorcade with a police escort, made him wait five minutes because only so many vehicles were permitted on the jetty at any one time and then had the cheek to say that this had nothing to do with him being local secretary of the other political party.

And myself who, after swilling endless cups of coffee with the refinery security men, quite truthfully answered no when the Inspector asked if I had had a cup of tea and went off for another break.

And a certain elderly PC who summed it all up when he said, 'I suppose it is better than working really'.

6: POUNDING THE BEAT

Getting a drink in Milford was a bit different to patrolling the Dale Beat. You couldn't use a civvy jacket, there was much more chance of getting reported and different tactics were required but we still managed it. We would normally only bother on night duty when a couple of pints during the first part of the shift really helped the night go by. Before closing time it was usually in through the back door and spend half an hour or so skulking in a cellar or back room but after 'shut-tap' it was a matter of choosing one of the two or three pubs where the landlord seemed to be totally nocturnal and using a series of secret knocks and taps on doors and windows to get into the bar. Usually we only stayed for a quick pint or two but very occasionally a real session would develop. I remember one night I went with Sergeant Charlie Morris into The Spirit Vaults almost opposite the police station in Charles Street at about half past eleven. Charlie had a permanent thirst and encouraged by the landlord we drank free beer and played darts literally all night. We didn't even get back to the station for our meal break and eventually rolled in just before the morning shift came in at 5.45am. It's quite a strange sensation to go home after 'working' all night and climb into bed well pissed.

As I said, Charlie was always thirsty and it was a very rare night duty when he didn't get his usual two or three pints of bitter. There were usually four of us on shift with him and every night one of us would be selected in strict rotation to be his drinking partner. He was quite happy for us to drink with him but he got a bit touchy if we indulged in a bit of free enterprise and sneaked a drink on our own or when it wasn't our turn. One night I was overtaken by a raging thirst around midnight. I had been out with Charlie the night before and remembering his route then I tried to work out which pub on my beat he was least likely to be in. Having given the appropriate coded tap on the window of the Three Crowns at Hubberston, I was ushered in and was halfway through my second pint when the same tap came again at the window and in came Charlie. The expected rollicking didn't materialise then or even later but for the rest of the week I was given the only beat that didn't contain a friendly pub or club.

A couple of years later I was on CID attachment and was 'sort of' on duty again in the Three Crowns and watched with interest as the landlord threw out a customer who was causing a few problems. The landlord at that time was well over six feet tall and well built with it and the customer was only small but knowing them both I expected a bit of a fight and was surprised when the customer left as quiet as a lamb without even an argument. The landlord was surprised as well and said as much after the man had gone. A full twenty minutes later, when everyone had moved on to talk and think about other things, there was a knock on the frosted glass service hatch of the off-sales counter. The landlord, expecting the usual small child looking for crisps or pop, opened the hatch and leaned through only to be met with an exceedingly solid punch on the nose from his small former customer. By the time he had recovered from the shock the little man was long gone. Together with several other regulars I was curled up with laughter for minutes and even the landlord eventually saw the funny side of it.

This brings a couple of other amusing incidents in pubs to mind. A middle-aged know-all of a customer asked for change of a pound (those were the days) and also asked for and was given precise directions to the cigarette machine. He marched purposefully across the bar and fed his fifty-pence piece straight into – the jukebox. The look on his daughter's face was unforgettable as she tried not to laugh and expressed the hope that he liked music because he had just bought twenty minutes-worth.

A job that was either loved or hated in the police force was enquiry desk duty often called SDO – Station Duty Officer. The disadvantages were that you couldn't hide from senior officers, couldn't combine walking your beat with shopping, couldn't tap on the back doors of pubs for a quick pint on night duty and couldn't call at nurse's homes or similar establishments for tea and sympathy and anything else that was going. Set against these were a number of advantages – time to catch up on your correspondence, produce underground magazines or anything else that required access to free stationery, the chance to have a smoke whenever you felt like one, the night time opportunity to rifle desks, read the Chief Inspector's confidential files or help yourself to the typist's toffees but best of all you were always warm and dry – I loved it.

PC Dai Williams had been at Milford for about ten years, something of a record and had spent much of that time on permanent SDO duty. One of his first tasks on nights would be to prepare reports and correspondence for transport to Headquarters later in the shift. Any sealed envelopes, especially those marked 'Staff Confidential' would draw him like a magnet and you could guarantee that within five minutes of being left alone in the station he would have the kettle on to steam them open. Knowing this a couple of us got together and prepared a report (signed by one of our better forgers in the name of the Chief Inspector) that suggested that PC Williams would greatly benefit from a posting to a station fifty miles away. We sealed the envelope, stamped it 'Confidential' and left it tucked among the rest of the correspondence for him to find, steam and read at his convenience. The posting we had suggested would not have been popular with even the keenest among us and when I returned to the station a couple of hours later I found Dai white faced, chewing his nails and prowling around like a caged tiger.

It was my turn to take the despatches to Headquarters and it was a simple matter to retrieve and destroy our confidential forgery before I delivered the rest. We kept things going for almost a week and thoroughly enjoyed watching Dai trying to draw out the Chief Inspector with 'casual' remarks about other people's postings and cunningly contrived references to the station in question. Eventually thinking he had suffered enough, we asked whether his posting had come through yet and the light slowly dawned. We stood back waiting for the explosion but he was too relieved to be annoyed.

Working the enquiry desk also meant operating the pocket radio control and some coppers were notoriously hard to contact if they thought that work could be involved. One particularly wily old campaigner was our resident mad Irishman Bill Lennon and I remember him really surpassing himself one day when the conversation went something like this:

'Control to PC518 - over'   -   Silence

'Control to PC518 - over'   -   Silence

'Control to PC518 - are you receiving - over'   -   Silence

'Control to PC518 - Come in Bill for Christ's sake. I only want to change the time of your meal break'   -   'Sorry control, I didn't receive your first three calls I must have a dud set'.

If you were on morning or day shift or if you were just visiting Milford Haven to pick up or deliver reports or documents, every effort was made to be in the station for the mid-morning break when there would be, at times, reasonably large gatherings in the canteen. I say canteen but it was just a fairly small room with not much more than a kettle, a toaster and a dart board by way of equipment. There could be useful exchanges of information but mostly it is the humour that I remember. For example:- The Chief Inspector with heavy sarcasm was saying that he felt 'out of it' because everyone else had got such long hair when a voice from the corner told him, 'Never mind Sir, your's will grow soon'. There was discussion as to why a particularly attractive young woman had very suddenly decided to move to the Midlands, ending when someone said, 'Perhaps she fancies a Coventry Climax'. A Sergeant, joining a discussion on a particularly exciting F1 Grand Prix race and having just completed a Vehicle Damage Report, 'I only hope the buggers on my shift didn't see it'.

Some humour was of the more unintentional kind. When an 18st Sergeant was elected to the Local Police Federation Committee, a young PC totally unaware, said, 'I'm glad Dai got on. He'll carry more weight than Charlie'. A WPC actually talking about shopping, 'I'm a bit tight really. I suppose it's the way I'm made.' Some though, was very well constructed – discussion on the arrest of a violent drunk, 'I suppose a bite on the hand is worth two in the mush'. A bored Sergeant having listened at length to a young man telling him that his qualifications included 'O' Levels in Woodwork and Welsh Language, 'Then the best thing you can do is bugger off home and make a Welsh dresser'. A toilet window had been broken during the night and there was much discussion as to the cause with the eventual conclusion being that it must have been wind. Voice from a different corner, 'If that was wind, I would hate to have his arse this morning.'

In those days, Milford Haven Marina was still Milford Docks and there were still a small number of trawlers landing fish and if a landing happened to coincide with finishing a night duty at 6am it was always worth a visit to the fish dock while the buyers were still around to pick up some cheap or even free fish. The free variety were normally dabs a bit too small for sale but very tasty. The Docks also had its own Dockyard Police – a Sergeant and a few Constables with basically the powers of Special Constables. They wore almost the same uniform as us but had no jurisdiction outside the dock boundary. They had a small office just inside the dock gates off Victoria Street opposite The Globe and Railway pubs which was always handy for shelter and a cup of tea on a cold wet night.

Anything serious however was still a matter for us and this reminds me of one of the best quotes ever. A Breton fisherman, doubtless drunk, had fallen into the dock and was missing presumed drowned. Some several days later having slept with the fishes for a while (and having been nibbled by them a bit), he surfaced and the Dockyard Police passed the problem to us. A colleague was sent accompanied by a young probationer to retrieve the body for post mortem and a Coroners report. The usual method of retrieving bodies that had been in the water a long time was to ease them gently onto a wire mesh stretcher. This they were attempting to do when the young probationer, rather than pulling on the man's clothing, grasped his hand which promptly came away at the wrist. Full of sympathy for the young man who had probably never even seen a normal dead body before, my colleague who shall be nameless said, 'I asked you to give me a hand not bloody take one'.

Talking of fish and on a happier note, once when working my own Dale beat, I was heading back from Milford with the luxury of driving an *Austin Mini-Van* (obviously no working motorbikes available) and was following a small lorry down Herbrandston Hill when a box fell off the back. I made a note of his registration number with thoughts of a very easy booking for 'Insecure load' and stopped to pick up the box. It was slightly damaged but pretty much intact and closer examination showed it was full of lovely fresh fillets of haddock. I made an instant decision that losing the box was probably punishment enough and let the truck carry on its way. Two freezers soon became rather full and fish was frequently on the menu for myself and my sister for quite a while.

7: *DALE DAYS*

Fires are never pleasant but they could provide some amusing moments. I was called out to a fire at a farm and by the time the fire appliances got there a Dutch barn full of hay or straw was well ablaze. There was nothing the firemen could do but keep it damped down and stop it spreading to other buildings. It was quite a cold evening and I stood with the farmer and the Fire Service Station Officer enjoying the warmth from the fire. We could see that a tractor inside the shed was practically burnt out and the Station Officer casually asked the farmer what else was in there. Our farmer, probably with a profitable insurance claim in mind began to reel off an endless list of bits and pieces and at the very last said, 'Oh yes and a jerry can of petrol and four or five *Calor Gas* cylinders'. I was about the last to realise just what he had said and must have come close to the Olympic 100 metres sprint record as I joined everyone else in the dash for cover. As it happened, the explosions when they came weren't too bad but I'm glad that we moved when we did - it just needn't have been that fast!

Another fire, this time at Dale, enabled me to get my own back on a few people who had been causing me some strife. It was at the height of the summer season and as usual I was having endless trouble with motorists who, possibly because they were town orientated and didn't see any double yellow lines or more likely because they were pig-ignorant and couldn't care less, left their vehicles wherever it suited them and without any regard for anyone else, particularly the local residents. The road leading down to Watwick Beach was always a problem as it was a private road where nobody could be booked for obstruction but which I had to try to keep open for farm vehicles, navigation light maintenance crews, Coastguards and other emergency services. One group of holidaymakers who seemed to drive to the beach with a car each had been a bloody nuisance for almost a fortnight and despite my continued requests and notes always parked so as to make it almost impossible for other larger vehicles to pass. Their cars and driving documents (all checked the first time I saw them there) were all in perfect order and they knew that I was beating my head against a brick wall and the buggers were quite enjoying it.

But chance intervened. A fire broke out in some gorse on the cliff top and the only access to the fire was along this stretch of road. I had been told by radio that a fire engine was on its way but I knew that it would take at least fifteen minutes to get there. Not long enough to find the drivers of the cars but quite long enough for what I had in mind. The local farm lads were as fed up as I was with the continual obstruction and it was no problem at all to arrange a tractor, a length of chain and an all too willing driver. All the cars in the way were towed none too gently into a nearby muddy field and by the time the fire engine arrived the road was totally clear. I was left to write polite little notes to all the drivers explaining how any damage to their cars may have been caused and reminding them that I had been telling them for days about the need for access for emergency vehicles. Not one complained. The fire would probably have burned itself out quite safely but with a lovely ironic twist it had been one of the holidaymakers who had dialled 999.

One of my local pubs had been troubled for days with what they thought was a smoky fire but with great powers of observation the landlady eventually noticed that unlike most fires, it carried on smoking after it had gone out. Expert advice was sought from a off-duty fireman who just happened to be passing and he no doubt thinking of the turn-out fee, decided that it was a job for the brigade. The local 'retained' crew was called out and with headlights blazing and blue lights flashing they managed to arrive at the pub without mishap. I had been called out as well and by a miracle of good timing the fire engine, me and opening time all arrived at precisely the same moment. Having established that a small fire was located within a beam above the fireplace and that it constituted no danger to the public or more importantly, the beer supply, they sat down to plan the operation with a free pint from the landlady to aid their thinking. I didn't need to think but as a pub regular got a free pint anyway.

The firemen eventually came up with a plan of action that involved the delicate removal of a few inches of plaster to get at the beam, extinguishing the fire and then damping down to ensure that it didn't flare up again followed by lengthy advice to the landlady about building repairs to prevent a further fire. As this was classified as a house fire I was justified in being present throughout and as the operation proceeded the beer continued to flow and the morning developed into quite a party. I must say that I was lost in admiration for the firemen for the way they tackled the job, the advice they gave, the way they cleared up all the mess they had made and the way that they finished all this exactly one minute after closing time.

Talking of smoke, (You'll see the link eventually),early in my time at Dale I received a report of an unexploded shell on Marloes Sands and was told that I should clear an area for a helicopter landing. I rode down the path on my motorbike as far as I could go and walked the rest finally locating an excited group of holidaymakers in a large circle around an object. It was grey and shell shaped and I saw no reason for closer examination with the military on the way. I got the crowd to move away a bit and form an even larger circle then recruited a couple of kids to help me make a big 'H' in the sand. The chopper arrived and the experts approached the 'shell'. Very quickly they called me over and showed me what it was – a

NATO smoke float. It looked like a shell but was made of wood with a metal rod up the middle and was very light (designed to float obviously). If it was light and the end was well blackened it had obviously discharged all its smoke and was perfectly safe. I reported back to HQ and told them not to call the military next time until I had had a look.

Over the years several more turned up, mostly at Marloes, and holidaymakers looked on in wonder when after a quick check, I picked the 'shell' up, tucked it under my arm and later pushed it into the pannier on my motorbike. I used to take them home and chop them up for kindling wood with the occasional sparks as my axe hit any residue of phosphorous (or whatever it was) and boy they burned well.

Another quite memorable false alarm was when a visitor reported human remains on a beach saying he had seen the bones of a hand close to the cliff. The location was a little cove around from West Dale accessible (just about) from Dale Airfield near The Hookses only at low tide. I recruited a couple of Coastguard Volunteer Cliff Rescue members, I think Dai Gainfort was one and they led me down a very interesting route to the sand. The man had marked the spot with a pile of large stones and we soon discovered the bones. Yes, it was a hand but when that hand belongs to a seal it's usually called a flipper. We gave the flipper a decent burial.

Sudden deaths continued to form part of life's rich pattern (well for me if not for them!). One day I was called to St Ishmaels where John Dillon, a former resident of the Brook Inn hadn't been seen for a few days and I got the job of breaking into his house in Lindsway Villas to investigate. This I did and found him dead in bed – a straightforward sudden death but with one small problem. The problem was John's dog that was sitting on his chest and threatening to take my arm off whenever I went anywhere near the body. I sent for a doctor to certify that the old boy was actually dead and while I waited for him to arrive I made several attempts to remove the dog. It was only a small Jack Russell type dog. Most dogs have never caused me a problem and I'm certainly not frightened of them but this one seemed to have been sent totally berserk by its master's death, was intent on protecting him and I just couldn't get near it.

The doctor arrived and our joint efforts to move the dog having failed, he made an exceedingly fast examination of the body while, armed with motorcycle gauntlets and a long handled broom, I pinned the dog against a wall. Having confirmed that our friend really was dead the doctor made an equally fast exit. Still left with the problem of separating John and his dog, I got some help from a neighbour and with the aid of the gauntlets, the broom and a large wet sack we finally trapped our loyal four-legged friend and locked him in the outside lavatory. This feat was not achieved without climbing on to the bed with the body and knocking poor old John's false teeth out in the scramble to throw the sack over the dog and keep it secure. The state of the house was fascinating but sad.

John had died in a back bedroom in a tatty bed with just old army blankets and an overcoat to cover him but in the front bedroom a double bed was beautifully made up and his late wife's clothes were laid out just as she had left them years before. On the landing and down the stairs every newspaper, every magazine and all the post that had ever come into the house were arranged in neat stacks five or six feet high. In the kitchen most of the floor space was covered with empty but relatively clean milk bottles. The house wasn't particularly dirty – I've definitely seen worse but it was just totally full with nothing ever having been returned or thrown away. In the end the doctor called to say that he was able to issue a death certificate so it wasn't a 'sudden death' and I needn't have been involved at all. Attending post mortem examinations was a part of the 'sudden death' routine that caused problems for some. Ashen faces and fainting were not unknown and one particular PC I knew would deliberately report sick on the day following dealing with a sudden death – just to avoid the PM. Only small children caused me any real upset and I have watched people I knew quite well being sliced up without any real problem. It was amazing though how often that Haidee, quite unaware that I had been to a post mortem that day, would serve up kidneys or liver for lunch or dinner but I was never one to waste good food. The examinations could be quite gruesome but I was very fortunate because many of those I attended were made more bearable, if not actually enjoyable, by the other (live) persons present. The mortuary attendant was one of these. His looks and the fact that I never saw him unless there was at least one dead body present made me think of Frankenstein's assistant Igor whenever I saw him but he was one of the friendliest and most cheerful men I have ever met.

He prepared the body for the pathologist and gave him a hand when any extra muscle was needed such as wielding a giant pair of secateurs to snip out the rib cage. He helped put everything back afterwards (the fact that the brain often went back where the stomach should have been didn't really matter) and then with a neat herringbone stitch from neck to navel or beyond, sewed the job up so to speak. Having assisted in the butchery department he would then exercise real loving care in dressing the body and making it so presentable that no friend or relative seeing it afterwards could ever suspect what it had been through. A man who can do that job day in day out for very little pay and still remain cheerful, friendly, helpful and courteous has my total respect.

The pathologist, Dr Hollick, was another real character. But for the fact that he suffered from slight epilepsy he would no doubt have been an excellent surgeon although he would freely admit that it was a lot easier operating when nothing needed to work after you had finished with it. He had a habit of talking out loud about what he found during his examination of the body and carrying on a separate conversation with you at the same time. On top of this he would occasionally suffer one of his epileptic episodes when he would stop talking, stand perfectly still for seconds or even minutes and then carry on with his conversation and with whatever else he was doing as if nothing at all had happened. Until you got used to it all this could be a bit disconcerting and a dialogue with him could go something like this:

'Had a lovely run up into the Cotswolds last weekend – pulmonary phyma, probably benign – beautiful weather for it – slight oedema of the colon – stopped for lunch at a lovely country pub – evidence of an earlier appendectomy – best pint ………..(2 minute gap) ……….. pint of ale I've tasted for a while – considerable thickening and distortion of the right ventricle – I'd like to go again if I can get leave - yes, that's what saw him off – trouble is finding a stand-in – look at these lungs, yours are just as dirty if you smoke – have you ever spent any time in the Cotswolds? – stomach contents indicate a meal about an hour before death – lovely area the Cotswolds – looks like, yes it's fish and chips'. and so on.

Dr Hollick was an incredible man and he did find a stand-in for one PM that I attended and that I shall always remember. The locum was obviously a very keen young man and thrilled to bits to get the chance to try his skill. He almost leapt up and down with excitement every time he found something and kept dragging me over to have a closer look at various bits of a very old lady. He was repeating, 'incredible', 'fascinating pathology' and 'any one of these three things could have killed her' all the way through the examination and I thought he was going to have a heart attack himself when he started slicing up the liver, 'Oh this is so rare, come and look at this, fantastic, she was infected with liver fluke, look, usually only find it in sheep, transmitted by dogs you know, probably lived on a farm as a child, look, look, see what I mean, you'll probably never see that again'. I didn't and to be honest I wasn't too bothered that I hadn't. Despite the number of not too welcome close up looks at the evidence, this PM was really interesting. The old lady had died a couple of days after suffering a fall at a care home for the elderly and probably much to the relief of the staff there our pathologist was able to prove it was what had killed her that had caused the fall and not the fall that had killed her.

Once following a PM on a suspected suicide, I was taking various organs for examination at the forensic science laboratory at Cardiff. I was in an unmarked car, it was a long trip and to ease the boredom I broke all regulations and picked up a hitch-hiker. We got into conversation and I must admit it faltered a bit when I told him the purpose of my journey. After a pause he asked me where all the lady's bits and pieces actually were. When I told him that her stomach was in the bag by his feet, he went deathly white and leapt out of the car at the next set of traffic lights without even thanking me for the lift – ungrateful sod!

The police couldn't operate without information from the public and although we didn't like it much a fair proportion of that information came anonymously, sometimes by letter. People went to great lengths at times to hide their identity, even going as far as cutting letters out of newspapers and sticking them on to sheets of paper one at a time. Despite all this, in the rural areas we very often knew exactly where and who they had come from. In one of my villages, a middle-aged bachelor (let's call him John because that was his name) was a regular in the pub and usually went home just before closing time. But every now and then he would rebel against petticoat government and have a spell of three or four nights when he would stay with the rest until the landlord threw them out. As soon as this happened you could guarantee that within a couple of days we would have an anonymous letter (from his sister) complaining about after hours drinking at the pub. I would duly make an official visit and having previously told the landlord that I was coming, would find everything in order and report accordingly.

Another lady was a regular correspondent and I usually immediately filed her anonymous epistles in the waste bin. Eventually she must have realised that this was what I was doing and took to writing direct to the Chief Constable. The letters still filtered down to me but I now had the inconvenience of having to type a report on the action I had taken. Such a source of extra work could not be allowed to continue so the next time I saw the lady in question in the crowded village shop I took the opportunity to tell her in a nicely audible stage whisper that I had received her latest letter. If looks could kill I wouldn't be here today but it had the desired effect.

Sometimes information came by anonymous telephone call, usually to one of the larger stations. On one summer evening Milford was short staffed and I was called in from Dale to man the enquiry desk and switchboard for half a shift. One of the first calls I took was an anonymous complaint and I immediately recognised the man's voice as that of one of my own 'parishioners'. He refused to say who he was and it gave me great pleasure when I told him that we would investigate his complaint to finish by calling him by his first name. He didn't know which way to look next time we met.

Another charming character was even worse. He would pass all sorts of snippets of information to me in a most friendly manner and then phone the Chief Inspector in Milford, tell him that he had told me and then hope that I would drop myself in it by taking no action. Fortunately the Chief Inspector usually told me that our friend had told him that he had told me (if you see what I mean). One evening I had been playing darts for the Lobster Pot somewhere at an away venue, we had won as was fairly usual and as was also fairly usual we had celebrated well. As our minibus driver brought us back towards Marloes through the country lanes we had to squeeze past a parked car and caught a glimpse of someone climbing back over the hedge probably having pinched a 'feed' of new potatoes.

Next morning the Chief Inspector told me that our charming friend (who was the minibus driver!) had reported me for not taking action on a theft in progress. Fortunately the boss didn't think it was unreasonable that having had a few drinks I had chosen not to leap from a moving bus to apprehend the spud thief especially as I had taken a note of his car registration. My 'friend' still had the gall to smile sweetly and chat away next time we met. There was some satisfaction though in knowing that his activities didn't go unnoticed locally. When I first moved to Dale I had mentioned my new 'friend', Mr R J Edwards of Talbenny Agricultural Workshops, to my darts mates and they said in unison, 'You mean Dick the Spy'.

Speaking of the Lobster Pot darts team, we were unique in the league in that we had a non-playing captain. Billy Price from St

Brides was much older than all the players but had a great knack of picking the right team, playing them in the right order and inspiring confidence. My team mates included Dai Howells, Pete Sturley, Danny Scale, Dai Gainfort, Anthony Scale and Vince Goffin. Vince was probably our best player but one season had a very bad case of the yips (aiming the dart but struggling to actually release and throw it). He fought through and beat the problem but didn't reach the same heights of form again.

Historically, Dale had been a village where the classes were set apart with Dale Castle and Allenbrook House having the vast expanse of Dale Meadow between them and the homes of the fishermen and farm labourers. This had been perpetuated to an extent by the RNAS which had built their married quarters with officers' detached homes in a neat crescent on the Castle side and the semi-detached houses of the other ranks on the opposite side of the meadow in Blue Anchor Way along with the council housing stock. But by the time we arrived, just about everybody mixed with just about everybody else.

The nearest thing we had to aristocracy were Mr & Mrs Hugh Lloyd Phillips of Dale Castle. I called to make myself known soon after arrival and was made most welcome. They were slightly remote but did play their part in the village. At Allenbrook were Mr Burnet Henry George Rind and his wife Beatrix. The family had run Dale Nurseries for many years and both Mr Rind and his father Lt.Col.George Burnet Abercrombie Rind had been High Sheriffs of Pembrokeshire but to the whole village they were Bunny and Beata who played a full part in village activities.

Through the Griffin, Margaret Fisher's shop, Dale Sailing Company, the Coronation Hall Committee, the Carnival

Committee and the W.I. We got to know many and came to call them friends. Some are lost in the mists of time but names that spring to mind in no particular order are Campbell & Mil Reynolds, Mona and Harry Llewellyn, Joy Griffiths, the Duffields, Beryl Dando, Dai Gainfort, Brian Thomas, the Copleys, Celia John, Audrey Oldham, Bob Medway and Anne Griffiths. I knew that I had fully become part of the community when the family asked me to be a pallbearer at the funeral of Jack Thoma

8: *MILFORD DAYS*

We had no garage at 77 Blue Anchor Way. In fact because the houses were built on a bank high above the road, only one house had a garage, dug into the bank and that looked awful. I had removed part of the front wall and created a ramp so that I could ride the motorbike up to park near the house but the car had to stay down on the grass verge. So it was that an idiot holidaymaker, looking behind to see if his boat trailer was still attached, managed to drive into the rear end of my *Hillman Imp* in the summer of 1972. He looked up at the last moment and in his words, 'tried to get in the gap between the wall and the car' (all of eighteen inches) and therefore managed to hit the nearside rear corner of the *Imp* and push it across to the other side of the road almost bringing the front offside into contact with the wall on that side.

Almost wasn't good enough because I had already caused some slight damage to that corner so I made sure that the damage had been freshened up with a hammer and a screw driver and that the car was resting right against the wall before the duty Sergeant arrived to fill in the accident report. The insurance sorted out the damage but I'd gone off the car by the time I got it back, so on 8 August we went to Nicholas's Garage in Haverfordwest and bought a maroon *Triumph Toledo* YDE 523K for £835 with £180 part-exchange on the *Imp*.

In the winter it was back into Milford Haven and the never-ending problem for Chief Inspector Brian Bebb of deciding what the hell to do with me. He solved the problem on one day at least by sending me on PSU training. It was about this time that we had already had the first miner's strike with some power cuts and problems on picket lines in other parts of the country so Police Support Units were being formed or re-formed. The theory was that a PSU consisting of about thirty specially trained men could be assembled quickly and transported to any area of the force or neighbouring forces that required assistance in numbers. Emphasis was placed on crowd control and the most likely use of a PSU would be at demonstrations and mass pickets. Hopefully in these days things have improved but then my specialist training that honed me into a high state of readiness lasted just that one very entertaining day!

There were four of us from the Milford Haven Sub-Division and as the chosen elite prepared to leave under the command of Inspector Davies, a young Inspector who had the rare distinction of being the holder of a George Medal for bravery (arresting an armed man), one glance was enough to convince me that we had been specially selected. The factors governing selection were obviously intelligence, physical fitness and what shift we were on that day – not necessarily in that order. After a fairly trouble-free run to Haverfordwest in the Inspector's ancient *Ford Corsair* we were ready to begin our training. First as always came the briefing, which was memorable if only for the fact that one of the senior officers present was heard to mutter, 'Silly buggers' at least twice – and that during a week when he was due to read the lesson in chapel on Sunday.

Following the briefing came a fascinating film that showed us how large numbers of Metropolitan Police Officers could easily control equally large numbers of Metropolitan Police Cadets in plain clothes who had obviously been told exactly what to do and how and where to do it in order to make the film look impressive. It was now time for more practical things and we went outside to spend hours learning how to en-bus, de-bus, trudge and wedge. A *Silcox Motors* coach had been specially hired for the occasion but getting on and off of the thing became less than interesting to say the least especially after you had got on and off at least fifteen times. This period was only enlivened by the occasional visitor to the station staring in disbelief at the sight of thirty policemen in full uniform leaping on and off a bus that was obviously going nowhere and by one of the Inspectors in charge who caused a certain amount of confusion by ordering us to 'en-bus' when we were already 'en', if you see what I mean.

Next came linking arms and forming cordons and wedges. I didn't enjoy the simple cordon as by a bad miscalculation in my positioning I found myself with a 6ft 4in ex-guardsman on one arm and a certain PC Owen who had only just made the qualifying height and was variously known as 'Cuddles' or 'Tweedledum' on the other arm. The result was that it was impossible to link my hands in front of me in the required manner without taking on a sharp list to starboard and half folding one leg like a flamingo with a bad attack of arthritis. From the cordon we progressed to the wedge and the highpoint of the day was seeing one of our patrol car drivers trudging forwards with a very determined look on his face. The only problem being that he was flanked by two much larger officers and as his feet moved perfectly in the approved trudging movement, they were at least six inches off the ground.

The wedge, led by an Inspector (from the rear, naturally) was an impressive sight and proved how a highly trained and coordinated body of twenty men could force its way through a crowd of at least ten (led by one of our number who played flank forward for Llangwm Rugby Club) at only the third attempt. Even then it was necessary for the Inspector to stage whisper, 'For

Christ's sake let them through this time boys, the Chief Super's watching'. So ended my PSU training which, if nothing else left me happy in the knowledge that we could get on and off a bus quicker than any team of flying pickets in the country.

Another wintertime occupation was attending a Senior Constable's Refresher Course, which compared to all other courses were very relaxed affairs. By the time you qualified for one of these you had finished your probation, passed or given up on promotion examinations, had enough service in not to let anything much worry you and were secure in the knowledge that there was no test or exam at the end of the week to see whether you had been listening. In fact if you had kept up reasonably well with changes in the law as they came along the only things to be gained from refresher courses were five days of total relaxation and about a stone in weight. My last two such courses were both at the Dyfed County Council residential education centre at Ferryside in Carmarthenshire where, Dyfed Council Tax payers be praised, the food would have done credit to a good class hotel.

The programme for a typical day would be something like this:- Early morning tea, (read the papers), choice of cereals, fried bacon, sausage, egg, tomato, fried bread, bread and butter, small mountain of toast, tea, (short break for lecture), coffee, biscuits, (another lecture), soup, vast quantity of croutons (mainly because nobody else at my table knew what croutons were), meat and two vegetables, desert, coffee, (further lecture or optional nap), tea and cakes, (final lecture), starter, meat and three vegetables, desert, cheese and biscuits, coffee, (short wait for pubs to open), eight or nine pints of lager, fish and chips, coffee (and so to bed). It was usually at least a fortnight before our uniforms fitted properly again.

The lager consumption caused some embarrassment one night. We were housed in single rooms in a two-storey living accommodation block and my room was at the furthest end of a very long corridor on the first floor. I woke in the early hours with an urgent need to visit the gents, which of course was not only at the other end of the corridor but also down on the ground floor. A swift calculation of the distance involved against the contents of my bladder told me that I would never make it. My first thought was the wash basin in the room but I would have to wash in that in the morning and the only other alternative was the window. My window overlooked the road and a railway line and having already spent three nights in the room, the times of the trains were etched in my memory and a quick look at my watch told me that there wasn't one due.

At two in the morning in a sleepy village I didn't expect too much pedestrian traffic so I opened the window, climbed up onto the sill and began to heave a huge sign of relief. I was in full flow when my eyes became accustomed to the light and I saw to my horror that a little old lady was walking her dog directly below me. All I could do was pull the curtain across my face and do my best impression of an overflow pipe. As the seconds ticked by it seemed that I had drunk more like ninety pints than nine and it felt like forever before I could leap back into the room and gently close the window. I waited all next morning for the inevitable summons to the office of the Chief Inspector (Training) but it didn't come and I shall never know whether it was because my impression of an overflow was so good, whether she didn't even notice or whether perhaps she enjoyed it.

Ferryside has two other memories that have stayed with me. Being in Carmarthenshire the village was still dry on Sundays but that posed no problems. When we checked in at the centre on the Sunday evening we were each handed a little card and a map. The map directed us to the local sailing club and the card was temporary membership of that club. With residential courses of some sort or another at the centre every week, the sailing club must have had the longest temporary membership list in Wales.

All of the other nights of the week there was a choice of two pubs and in one of these one night it came very close to the police being called to a fight between the police and the police! It was all about the Welsh speakers from Pembrokeshire getting annoyed that the Welsh speakers from Carmarthen and Cardigan were speaking Welsh when they were in company with non-Welsh speakers from Pembrokeshire, from Mid Wales and from England. The laugh was that the non-Welsh speakers couldn't have cared less, especially those from England but it got quite heated between both sets of Welsh speakers and blows were actually exchanged. The landlord was about to dial 999 but we managed to talk him out of it (in English).

I don't speak Welsh – well only a few words and most of those equivalent to four letter ones in English and it was never a problem as Dale and Milford Haven were in the half of Pembrokeshire that Welsh had never penetrated – the 'Little England beyond Wales' although no-one liked that description. But even there the noisy minority made sure that the silent majority had to put up with such vital facets of Welsh culture as bi-lingual tax discs, MOT Certificates, TV Licences and of course road signs. It didn't matter that a place had never had a Welsh name; they made one up and couldn't always agree among themselves what it should be (Milford Haven had never been anything other than Milford but got called both Milfordd and Aberdaugleddau according to how the mood took them). The Welsh name was stuck above the English name on road signs making them twice as big, twice as expensive and ten times more dangerous and confusing for the average motorist. But apart from this, my contact with the lunatic fringe was fairly minimal.

Before the bi-lingual signs became virtually universal throughout the Principality, the Welsh Language Society organised a campaign of stealing, smashing and defacing English only signs and when they had the bad luck to meet up with a local copper who wasn't a sympathiser or even a fellow member, they occasionally got caught. A number were due to appear in court in Carmarthen and as some sort of demonstration was expected, three of us from Milford Haven were drafted in as reinforcements.

We arrived to find a large and fairly vocal crowd outside the court dancing on a heap of smashed road signs, burning Union Flags and performing various other quaint tribal customs. We reported to the officer in charge at the courthouse who asked one or two pertinent questions, heaved a sigh of quiet resignation and sent us all away to lose ourselves for a couple of hours in a nearby pub. With either their usual efficiency or with an unexpected flash of humorous genius (I never found out which), our senior officers had managed to send to a Welsh only court in a Welsh speaking town with defendants, demonstrators and supporters all steadfastly refusing to speak anything other than Welsh, a lad from rural Leicestershire, A Scotsman with an Italian mother and me.

When the National Eisteddfod came to Haverfordwest, Welsh speaking coppers were drafted from all over the Dyfed Powys force area but they couldn't avoid using us ignorant monoglots for at least part of the time so we were all very carefully briefed as to what we should do if we were approached in the street by someone speaking Welsh. We were supposed to say (in Welsh), 'sorry I CANNOT speak Welsh' and on no account were we to risk upsetting anyone by saying that we DID NOT speak Welsh. Such careful briefing was bound to produce results. I was on patrol with a local Pembrokeshire lad and we very soon met our first all Welsh enquiry. My friend listened to the long monologue with an interested, caring expression and then said, 'if it's important speak English – if it's not, f*** off'. Our enquirer f***ed off. I eventually learned a few phrases in the language. One of the easiest and most useful is, 'dydw i ddim yn deall' (I do not understand) followed closely by, 'wnewch chi siarad yn araf' (will you speak slowly), 'dim siarad Cymraeg' (I DO NOT speak Welsh) and finally, probably in desperation, 'byddwch yn dawel' (be quiet).

Mention of court earlier reminds me that, just as had been the case in Huntingdonshire, the Clerks to the Courts in Pembrokeshire could be real characters at times. I was giving evidence in a fairly complicated drugs case and had placed before the court a notebook we had found in the defendant's car and which contained a complete script for the explanation they would give if they were found in possession of the drugs we had caught them with. The drugs and the notebook having both been found, they changed their explanation to an even more plausible one and there was the distinct possibility that they would get away with it. I particularly remember the case because I was attached to CID as an Aide and it was the first time I had given evidence in court not wearing a uniform. I was halfway through my story about finding the notebook in the car when our friendly Clerk interrupted me and with a look of angelic innocence said, 'I think their worships may be confused here Officer. Does this explanation they had prepared relate to this case or the one at my other court last week?' The Chairman tried not to smile, the defence solicitor tried no to groan too loudly and the druggies got well and truly done.It was a rule at court that witnesses in a case must remain outside the courtroom until they were called so as not to be influenced by what had gone before. A detective had given very detailed evidence in a particular case that lasted over an hour. His Sergeant was then called and started going through the whole lot again. Our Clerk with a pointed look at his watch suddenly stopped him and said, 'no doubt you have been listening at the door Sergeant; can you corroborate everything the Detective Constable has said?' The DS promptly replied, 'yes sir' and we all got to the pub an hour earlier.

Something that always caused problems in court were 'verbals'. In other words (and quite often they were literally other words) what a prisoner had said or was supposed to have said during an interview or at the time of his arrest and that weren't included in the written statement he had made (or refused to make) after he had had time to think about it. We were of course supposed to caution prisoners that they were 'not obliged to say anything' etc. so your evidence of incriminating verbals would normally be along the lines of, 'before I could caution him he suddenly said, OK I took the bloody thing'. Such verbals were always strongly contested on a 'Not guilty' plea and the defence would question at great length your memory, your veracity or even your parentage. An old lag once caused me endless trouble in court. When I arrested him he actually said, 'It's a fair cop guv'. Can you imagine the fun the defence solicitor had with that one – 'Officer do you really expect the court to believe that my client used such a phrase?' 'Are you sure you haven't been watching too much television?' etc. etc. The old devil very nearly got away with it.

But of course, it wasn't all work and I remember one day out which, if not typical was certainly memorable. Memorable enough to have merited a full report in the *Milford Mercury*. I can do no better that produce it word for word:-

SPORTS NEWS.

On Saturday March 10th at the unearthly hour of 7.15am, a minibus left Milford Haven making for the International at Cardiff. Among the party were such illustrious gentlemen as Mr Howell Williams R.F.C & bar, Mr Ieuan 'Cuddles' Owen, Mr George 'Double Top' Jackson. Mr Rod 'Odd Job' Evans and Mr John Rees, Rugby correspondent of Tennis News and Wisden.

All went well until the bus reached the outskirts of Llanelli, when two calamities struck. The first came to light as the bus was streaking down a hill at 70mph and it was noticed that the driver had gone very quiet and deathly white. This was a condition that described every passenger when it was learned that the brakes had failed. The second came when having somehow safely reached Llanelli and eventually finding the only garage open, it was discovered that we were far too early for the pubs to be open.

The garage had no parts, no skilled mechanic and no knowledge of Ford Transits but it did have a small apprentice with a large tool box. The party's mechanical knowledge did not total much but was at least ten times that of the unfortunate lad. After much helpful advice from all and much skilful persuasion of the apprentice to move over and let us have a go, the job was eventually completed under the direction of Rod Evans A.M.I.Mech.E. By this time the garage boss had arrived and immediately sacked his apprentice for taking on the job in the first place. He was eventually re-instated after powerful arguments – totally true, that he had not had much choice in the matter.So three hours and several cans of beer from the supermarket later, the mini-bus was once more on the road to Cardiff. The remainder of the journey was uneventful apart from the whole party strolling into a Rolls Royce showroom just to use the toilets and the gems of wit hurled at pedestrians by Howell Williams as we passed. Once in Cardiff, the party decided to replenish its energy after the rigours of the journey. Some did this by several beers and a visit to a strip club, some by a bottle of wine and a mixed grill and one by a bottle of wine and two more bottles of wine. And so to the match.

Little is known of what happened at the game itself as the party was split up singly or in pairs throughout the ground according to where the tickets acquired from various sources allowed entry. Mr Jackson was however heard to air his vast knowledge of Rugby Union with such comments as. "They can't start yet, they haven't got the nets on the goals' and muttering 'Foul' and 'Handball' until he was intimidated into silence by an immense and hairy Welshman shouting 'Cymru Cymru Cymru' some six inches away from his ear at intervals of about ninety seconds throughout the whole match.

After the game, the party gathered in the Royal Hotel where in an endeavour to forget the price of the beer they drank more than several pints of it and eventually managed to get almost the whole bar singing and enjoying such sport as setting fire to a newspaper as it was being held up and read by someone not joining the choir. It says much for the quality of the beer that at one stage of the proceedings, Mr George Jackson was heard not only singing but singing in pidgin Welsh. From Cardiff to Swansea and more liquid refreshment and eventually the drive home when nothing was heard but the swishing of the tyres, the *gentle snoring of Howell Williams and the sighs of 'Cuddles' Owen as he sat hugging a fur coat across his knees and gently stroking it now and then. A day well spent and I think Wales won.*

9: *MR FIXIT ?*

On 1 January 1973 we joined the Common Market as the European Community was then known, three months later we experienced the first 'benefit' of entry as we started to count the cost of a newfangled tax called value added – VAT. But it was on Wednesday 5 August that year that something happened that had much more effect on the Dale, Marloes, St Ishmaels area and this is one story that I really can start with, 'It was a dark and stormy night'.

Mum and Dad were staying with us and I had taken them to the Brook Inn at St Ishmaels. Haidee stayed at home in Dale with the boys. It was heading towards closing time and by then it really was a dark and stormy night and lashing down with rain. I was about to order another round when I was told there was a telephone call for me. It was one of the Sergeants from Milford Haven who told me that a tanker had run aground in Lindsway Bay, it was leaking badly, wind was blowing petrol fumes into the village, Most of St Ishmaels had to be completely evacuated and I was on duty NOW to help do just that.

Someone offered to take Mum and Dad back to Dale, Malcolm Rowlands, the landlord lent me a set of oilskins because I had no wet weather gear with me. Some police were already in the village. I made a rendezvous with them at Lindsway Villas and we split the village up for evacuation. Now picture the scene. You are getting ready for bed or are already there, it is dark, blowing a gale and pouring with rain. Suddenly there is a knock at your front door and you open it to see that someone has arrived in a maroon *Triumph Toledo* with no markings or blue lights and a man, reeking of lager and dressed in bright yellow waterproofs is trying to tell you in an English accent that not only is he really a policeman but that you have got to get out of your home immediately.

As you can imagine, some took a bit of persuading, some we never even found and one at least, Dai 'Pink Panther' Jones, steadfastly refused to move saying that if he was going to die, he'd die in his own f***ing bed and leaving his wife and kids no choice in the matter. Eventually, well into the early hours, it was decided that we had done as much as we could and it was time for us to remove ourselves from the possibility of being blown up. I can honestly say that I was so busy waking people up, persuading them to listen and getting them to go (go where? – we couldn't tell them) that the thought of being blown sky high myself never even entered my head. As I wasn't really on duty, wasn't in uniform and was still half pissed, I was allowed home for a few hours sleep. The following day, most of the fumes had blown away, people were allowed back into their homes and it began to become clear what had happened.

A Greek owned Liberian registered tanker the *Dona Marika* had been at anchor in the Haven with apparently nobody on watch or even awake. It had broken from its moorings and run onto rocks off Lindsway Bay, which had sliced it open like a sardine can spilling 3,000 tonnes of aviation fuel into the sea. By the following morning, you could still smell the fumes in the village but it was safe to light a cigarette (I did hold my breath a bit when I lit my lighter!). However on or near the ship itself smoking or even a slight spark was not an option. It would require an expert salvage crew to deal with the wreck and within a few days such a crew led by Scotsman Gordon Fraser began to assemble and the St Ishmaels area started what would become a financial bonanza for many and something similar to a gold rush in the Wild West of Wales. Salvage experts came in earning and spending big money, locals were employed on the salvage and as drivers or general dogs-bodies and Malcolm Rowlands did very nicely as The Brook became Gordon Fraser's evening venue for management meetings, meals and hard drinking.

As both a regular at The Brook and village bobby I was soon recruited by Gordon as a source of knowledge of the, 'Who's got one of those?' or 'Who do I see about that?' and the, 'Can I trust him?' variety. In return he became the source of a fair quantity of free lager but he and his crew were excellent company and I did buy a few rounds myself. One evening Gordon asked my advice. One of his men had been stop checked driving a vehicle hired to the company and had elected to produce his driving documents to me at Dale unfortunately he wasn't on the list of approved drivers submitted to the hire company and this would invalidate the insurance. Both the driver and the company would be liable and the company would be likely to get a fairly massive fine. After a bit of thought I suggested that if the driver was willing we could say that he thought he had permission to drive the car as an employee but the company hadn't given him that permission so it would be a very technical 'Taking without consent'. He would get a much smaller fine and a slap on the wrist and Gordon would pay the fine.

The driver was willing and so the following day I met him by arrangement, arrested him and charged him with the offence. He was from Cardiff and was a brother of Emile Ford (who with *The Checkmates* had a number one hit with *What Do You Want To Make Those Eyes At Me For* in 1959 and two more top tens in the following year). The case went to court a few weeks later when I was horrified to discover that the idiot driver hadn't bothered to tell Gordon or me that he had a string of previous

MV Dona Marika (when without a hole in the bottom)

driving convictions including one for taking a motor vehicle without consent! He would be very lucky not to go to prison and this time he was totally innocent. I told him to plead 'not guilty' so that I would have to give evidence and then, after I had done my bit, to change his plea to 'guilty' and ask the court for leniency. I went into the box and really laid on with a trowel the fact that I was totally satisfied that he really thought he had permission to drive the vehicle and that it was all a big misunderstanding (not difficult when he really had been instructed to take the trip). The Magistrates were 'out' for ages and when they came back the Chairman said that they had seriously considered a custodial sentence but had taken note of the mitigation detailed by the arresting officer and a fine would suffice.

Gordon paid the fine there and then and was obviously very grateful as next time I saw him in The Brook he pushed something into my top pocket and said, 'Take your wife out for a meal'. When I got home and examined the contents of the pocket I found that the 'meal' was very nearly a week's wages. The salvage job was long and complicated – in simple terms they had to get rid of all the residual fuel and fumes, seal the holes with quick drying marine cement, pump out the water and tow her away (eventually to Falmouth for scrap). Gordon and his gang were around therefore for some considerable time and during these many weeks we got to know each other quite well and I did a number of further 'good turns' for him including spotting an employee who was ripping him off (quietly sacked and no paperwork for me).

I was still very much taken aback though when shortly before he was due to leave the area he offered me a job. He wanted me to travel the world with him to wherever the next job was, to troubleshoot, to do local liaison, to solve problems, to be his 'Mr Fixit'. I was earning £2,380 in 1973-74 and he was offering £5,000 a year plus bonuses and allowances! We thought long and hard but in the end I said no. Bill was only ten and Doug seven, we had only been in Wales a couple of years and at that time I had only ever been abroad once on a school trip to Switzerland. It would have been a giant step but I often wondered 'what if?' As it transpired, Gordon died not many years later so I possibly made the right decision.

So in the end I didn't change my way of life but there were no hard feelings and when he left Gordon presented me with a large mounted photograph of the *Dona Marika* and another 'meal'. Years later, in 1978, when I had changed my life (twice) and we were running The Brook ourselves, with the photograph of the *Dona Marika* Gordon had given to Malcolm Rowlands still hanging on the wall of the bar, there was another reminder and another bonanza. During the time that Gordon and his gang had been in virtual residence at The Brook, I had been called officially one night when one of his inner circle had had his wallet stolen. I was nearby at the time of the 'shout' and got to The Brook very quickly to take details and make unsuccessful enquiries.

All those years later Bill's eagle eyes spotted a wallet in the base of the hedgerow outside the pub. It had obviously been there for a very long time and the contents had almost totally rotted away but still there were the metal strips from a large number of banknotes. It seems likely that my early arrival that night had panicked the thief into dumping the wallet contents and all. We sent those contents off to the Bank of England and Bill ended up £66 better off – the very last of the *Dona Marika* gold rush.

In my description of the *Dona Marika* evacuation I mentioned Dai 'Pink Panther' Jones. Perhaps I should explain how he got his nickname. He was into 'jalopy racing', which was quite popular at that time in Pembrokeshire and involved stripped-out old bangers being raced round a grass track on friendly farmer's fields. Dai had very little success until he turned up at the track one day with a new car, a battered *Austin 1100*, hand-painted pink and christened *The Pink Panther*. He began to win a lot of races. This led to inevitable jealousy and suspicion on the part of the previous winners and I was tipped off that there was something very dodgy about the car. I enlisted the help of the Traffic Department's stolen vehicle specialist and went to look at the motor. It didn't take long to ascertain the original colour or that Dai had not even tried to obliterate the identification number stamped into the bodywork – perhaps he didn't even know that every car had one. From the number we would have been able to get the car's day of manufacture and track its registration via the dealer it was sent out to but Dai confessed long before then and led us to all the seats and equipment he had stripped out from the car and even the number plates of what was indeed a stolen vehicle.

The most interesting thing was that we also discovered that the *Austin* was a *1300* and not an *1100*, which apart from the relative newness of the car was why he had been winning so many races. If he had entered it as a *1300* he would probably never have been grassed-up and we would almost certainly never have traced that car. Later he had a legitimate road car with a large Welsh dragon emblazoned on the bonnet, which prompted this little entry in the *Milford Mercury*:

PROVE SOMETHING?

List of persons with large red dragons painted on their cars:

1. David Melfryn Jones (CRO) of St Ishmaels

2. Jeffrey Thomas (CRO) of Little Haven

3. Michael Davies (PC) of Milford Haven Police Station

Everything seemed very tame after the *Dona Marika* was towed away and life went back to normal with me back in Milford for the winter but there were still incidents to liven things up. A very large pig, in fact a quite nasty boar, escaped from its owner one day and was running amok among the traffic and causing general chaos around the town centre. Two of the lads were sent to see if they could catch it but all they succeeded in doing was making the animal even more wild and driving it out over the bridge towards Hubberston. It was foaming at the mouth, was obviously a real danger to the public and nobody knew what to do next. The situation was finally saved by the landlord of the Three Crowns pub who grabbed a shotgun and promptly shot the pig dead. The landlord's heroic and timely action received considerable coverage in the local press and there were great celebrations at the pub. Unfortunately all the publicity attracted attention from upon high and the end result was that one of the coppers who had failed to catch the pig but had happily joined in the celebrations at the Three Crowns was given the job of telling the landlord that he was being booked for not having a Shotgun Certificate and for discharging a firearm on the highway.

I was not a great fan of the breathalyser and thought it would probably be a bit hypocritical to use one as I would often have failed one myself coming home from darts matches at the Lobster Pot or from trips to The Brook or even on duty sometimes. Generally then I would only use the dreaded bag if I came across a driver who was so pissed that I would have arrested him under the old drink-driving law anyway. I came across one such as this on an evening patrol around one of Milford's industrial estates. I had followed his car as it had hit kerbs on both sides of the road leading into the estate. It eventually hit one too hard and stalled and the occupants were trying to push start it when I pulled up alongside.

The driver was a young boy who was so drunk he could hardly stand. His girlfriend wasn't much better and they both freely admitted that he had been the driver and that he had perhaps had, 'a drop to drink'. It almost seemed a waste of time to give him a breath test. From the state he was in it seemed more likely that the tube would explode rather than just turning green but I religiously went through all the procedures. He gave me a very good full length 'blow' but nothing happened, the reading was negative. We were allowed to have another go if we thought that a tube could be faulty so I rigged up another one, got him to blow again and still got the same result. The crystals stayed resolutely yellow – there wasn't even a tinge of green.

What I should have done then was to resort to the old legislation and arrest him anyway but by then it was only about fifteen minutes before I was due to go off duty at 10pm and the smell of his breath had begun to make me feel a bit thirsty myself. I locked the car, told them both to stagger home and collect the keys from the police station the following day. When I came back on duty the next afternoon I had nothing much to do and out of idle curiosity I ran a check on our drunken friend. He had a string of convictions as long as your arm, was on the run as an absconder from Borstal and was wanted for several burglaries committed during the time he had been out. Needless to say, he didn't call to collect the keys and I had missed arresting a certain Mr 'Smiler' Phillips who was well known locally but not to me because he had been 'away' whenever I was working Milford.

A few days later we received information that he was living on a caravan site locally and purely by chance I was the one who went with Sergeant Alex Jenkins to check this out. As we drove into the site we saw him go into the caravan in question so we knew he was in there. A different girl friend answered our knock and invited us in. She admitted that 'Smiler' had been there but wasn't there now. Looking around it was obvious from the lay-out of the van that the only place he could possibly be was under the bed/settee. Alex caught my eye and said to the girl, 'We'll wait 'til he gets back then' and promptly sat on the bed. I joined him and suggested that Smiler's friend could make us a cup of tea while we waited. She obliged and we sat enjoying both the tea and the fact that we were probably causing him considerable discomfort by sitting above him if not even literally on him.

Eventually we finished our tea, got up as if to leave and Alex said, 'OK Smiler you can come out now'. He did straight away and almost seemed relieved when I arrested him. I waited for some comment about our earlier meeting but either he was too drunk to remember or was so grateful for his few extra days of freedom that he never said a word. Not that long afterwards, he was released and was killed when his car left the road and crashed onto the track at the railway bridge at Steynton. The cynical would probably say that I did the world a service by missing the chance to get him disqualified again and allowing him to get himself killed but I am a great believer in fate and when your number's up it's up.

As ever I wangled as much time as possible in the warm and dry and got enquiry desk duty whenever I could. I was on this duty one day when a gentleman from the west of Ireland called to collect the belongings of his brother who had been killed in an accident on a construction site. A very sad occasion but bringing one of the funniest responses I had ever heard. I was trying to find out who exactly was his brother's next-of-kin and eventually discovered that he was divorced but did have one son. When I asked how old the son would be Paddy replied, 'Well I haven't seen him for twenty years – he must be all of eighteen by now'.

Looking after temporary residents in the cells was another facet of desk duty and this could sometimes provide some light entertainment. At Milford all prisoner's meals were collected from Rabaiotti's Café further down Charles Street. They did very good food and normally having had to make do with just sandwiches myself, the plate was often very much lighter by the time it reached the cell. Meals were also a way of getting back at any prisoner who was being a nuisance or who was in for anything particularly nasty. I have seen Epsom salts mixed in with the mashed potato and prisoners often contentedly munched their way through such delicacies as chicken, mushroom and fag ash pie or baked beans and *Lux* soap flakes on toast.

Drunks were often the main source of entertainment. One gentleman from the Emerald Isle was brought in drunk and incapable and smelling like a sewer for the third night in a row. When we checked-in his property and counted his money (for the third time) we worked out that at the current rate of expenditure he had enough for at least another two nights drinking. Something obviously had to be done. Every half hour he was woken up, stripped naked and taken out into the yard for ten minutes of gentle treatment with car shampoo, a (fairly soft) brush and a hosepipe. By the time he was bailed out at five-thirty in the morning he was shining white, wrinkled like a prune and absolutely determined not to spend another night at our particular 'hotel'. We never saw him again.

Conducting station breath tests after a positive roadside test was another part of desk duty and if it was positive offenders then had the choice of giving a blood or urine sample. Most chose to give a blood sample and a doctor would then be sent for. Opting to give a urine sample was extremely rare but one night after having taken the piss out of the Irish for years, I was punished by having to literally do just that!

10: *HAPPY CHRISTMAS !*

On 19 February 1974 Arthur Scargill started the main miner's strike and signalled the beginning of the end for Britain's coal industry. Having become a highly trained member of a Police Support Group (remember that one day with a bus at Haverfordwest), I was ready to be sent off to fight miners on a picket line in somewhere black and horrible. But I never got the call and Maggie Thatcher eventually beat the strike without my help but not before a lot of coppers suffered a lot of aggro. Later that month I got a message that Gran Maud was in Luton & Dunstable Hospital and not expected to come out. I went up on my next days off to see her telling the story that I had been sent up to Bedford on prisoner escort. She didn't believe a word of it but pretended that she did and I was glad to be able to spend a few last hours with her. Maud died on 6 March 1974 aged 78 and I had lost not just a grandmother but also a good friend who had taught me a lot.

It is interesting to compare the bill from S A Bates & Son for the funeral, which totalled £136.59 compared with the £15 and a few pennies charged for Maud's mother Lizzie. What didn't change at all was the fact that the bill was once again paid in full the day after it was issued. There was a funeral service at All Saints Houghton Regis and the Vicar Les Blackburn, was very kind to the family and conducted an excellent service. Cremation followed at Luton Crematorium and as Maud had always loved Wales both North and West so much it was decided that the Church cemetery at Dale should be her final resting place. I made all the necessary arrangements including interment of the ashes by Milford undertaker Frank Newing and Frank phoned me one day to say, 'Hello George the post has just come and Gran's arrived'. With all her years of association with undertakers as a layer-out of the dead, Maud would have really appreciated his matter-of-fact approach. Some time before I had seen an inscription on a gravestone that seemed very appropriate and I chose it for Maud's stone – *She lived for those she loved and those she loved remember. So*, Gran Maud had come to live in Pembrokeshire as well.

Not long after Maud's funeral, sister Jennifer having separated from husband Paul decided to move to Pembrokeshire with her by now six children Maxine, Helen, Paula, Stuart, Karl and Rachel. We found her temporary accommodation next door to us at 79 Blue Anchor Way in the holiday home owned by Pat and Bill Cannell. From there she went to a cottage at Dale Hill owned by Elwyn and Megan Bryan where she stayed for a while in company with vast numbers if mice, next back to Blue Anchor Way, to The Castle (a farm house) at St Ishmaels owned by John Llewellin and then to Milford Haven before finally settling in Neyland. So the tribe had begun to gather.

I was still getting involved in other people's sudden deaths and funerals. An old lady had died peacefully at home in bed but because she hadn't seen a doctor for some time it was treated as a sudden death and she had to go to the mortuary for post mortem. Fortunately the family had already called in an undertaker and he had agreed to transport the body provided that I gave his man a hand. The stairs were very steep and very narrow with a sharp turn half way up and we knew that we would probably have a bit of a problem with the 'shell' (lightweight coffin used for collections). We tried but in the end we found that we couldn't even get it up the stairs empty so we resorted to a flexible canvas bag especially designed for such situations.

Maxine on the zip wire in our garden in Dale with Bill & Douglas flanking Rachel, Karl & Stuart looking on & Douglas helps with the washing

When we loaded her into the bag we found that the old lady was not at all heavy and full of over-confidence we set off down the stairs. As I was only 'lending a hand' I had let the undertaker's young apprentice go first and needless to say as we negotiated the bend in the stairs, his hands slipped and we dropped her. The bag and its contents landed at the bottom of the stairs with a loud thud and a barely audible grunt right at the feet of a group of sorrowing relatives who had gathered near the front door to wish her farewell. The sight of the undertaker's lad trying to retain his dignity and his obvious respect for the dead as he climbed over the body to get into position for picking it up again was really something to see.

When we finally lifted the bag our second mistake became patently obvious. Because the old lady had been so light we hadn't bothered to fasten the retaining straps inside the bag and she had slipped. The undertaker's apprentice had all of the body at his end and my end of the bag was empty. He was about a foot shorter than me and I can only guess what we looked like as we scurried back towards the hearse. All I could think of at the time was the body snatchers Burke and Hare beating a hasty retreat from a graveyard. I saw him off and climbed in to my car to meet him at the mortuary. If the family saw my shoulders shaking as I drove away I can only hope that they thought I was overcome with emotion and not as it really was, maniacal laughter.

When I first thought about writing this book someone said, 'You'll have to have a bit of sex in it' and suggested that as there had been *Confessions of a Window Cleaner* and *Confessions of a Driving Instructor* there would be nothing wrong with *Confessions of a Clapped-out Ex-Copper*. After a bit of memory dredging though it seems that all those that offered I never fancied and all those I fancied never offered; so believe it or not (and I don't care if you do or not) there's not much to confess.

Fairly typical of the offers was Christine. She lived in the 'Ghaza Strip' on the Hakin council estate and I called on her one evening with a Distress Warrant for non-payment of a £5 fine. A young girl doing a passable impression of *Orphan Annie* opened the door and told me that her mother was, 'through there'. Through there proved to be a toilet where I found Christine surrounded by a cloud of gin fumes, stark naked on the floor with her head in the lavatory pan. We carried on quite a long conversation with me leaning against the door frame trying to look nonchalant and doing my best to look her in the face now and again rather than at all the other parts that were very much in evidence now that she had struggled into a position, still on the floor but sitting facing me. We eventually established that she had no money and that the next stage of the proceedings would be for me to stick a label on (destrain) something in the house worth a fiver or so.

Christine had recovered slightly by now. She found a dressing gown, almost put it on and we set off on a tour of the house with Christine clinging to me very tightly (and very pleasantly) for support. Under the terms of a Distress Warrant you had to exclude bedding, wearing apparel and tools of the trade – and everything on rental or hire purchase so we soon came to the inevitable conclusion that there was nothing in the house worth £5 and then the almost equally inevitable suggestion, 'What about me darling. I must be worth a fiver surely'. She started making us a cup of coffee while I thought about it. Christine was about twenty-five, blonde (well almost) and with the sort of body that wouldn't have looked out of place on page three of *The Sun*, especially the top half (top half of the body not top half of the page that is).

Eventually after some lingering looks at the several parts of Christine that were still available for viewing, I settled for just the coffee. I don't like the taste or the smell of gin and my mind kept going back to how I had found her with her head down the pan – not very conducive to sexual fantasy and anyway I only had three quid to last me for the rest of the week. I still wondered whether I had been wise or a bloody idiot when I got back to the station and endorsed the warrant, 'Nothing of sufficient value to destrain'. I had to call on Christine almost a year later. She was clean, sober and even better looking but that time she had the money!

Coming across scantily dressed females was not an everyday occurrence but it was surprising how often it did happen. One of my regular calls was on a family, which was so large that the council had given up trying to find a house big enough and had converted the disused school at Talbenny for their personal use. The old school was in the middle of nowhere but this didn't stop at least one member of the family getting into some sort of bother almost weekly. I would normally be greeted by the lady of the house who would say, 'F***ing hell, you again – which one do you want this time'. I would tell her and she would hold a roll call to try and establish which of her almost twenty children had left home, was a guest of Her Majesty or was just missing. If the one I was looking for was found, mother would grab them by the hair, irrespective of sex, age or size, place them in front of me, slap them soundly round the ear and say, 'Tell the man the f***ing truth'.

I called one evening and was given my usual seat in the kitchen while the roll call took place. One of the teenaged daughters was washing her hair in the kitchen sink stripped to the waist. She was the best looking of the bunch by far and as she stood up from the sink I could see that she had a most impressive pair of lungs. She was obviously well aware of my passing interest and standing only an arms length away she started drying her hair with a towel with slow sensuous movements and with 'come on' signals going at full strength. I had always thought that more than a handful was a waste but was rapidly beginning to change my mind when mother shattered all my lustful thoughts with, 'Cover your udders up girl it ain't f***ing milking time'.

Weirdly, in my most memorable encounter absolutely nothing happened. Something had been reported at Martin's Haven and I decided to go and have a look. I left my motorbike in the car park and started to walk down towards the sea. For some reason I had decided to polish my long motorcycle boots and wash the flies off my crash helmet and both were gleaming. It was a lovely day and I was in a short-sleeved shirt and epaulettes and looking uncharacteristically tidy. As I walked down the steep path, I saw a girl walking up towards me. She was wearing shorts and a fairly clingy loose sleeveless top with very obviously no bra underneath. She had gorgeous hair, was very good looking and had an absolutely stunning figure. As we approached each other, our eyes met and I knew that she knew exactly what I was thinking and I knew that she was thinking just the same about me As we passed each other we both broke into huge smiles. Not a word was spoken and I never saw her again but the memory all these years later is still vivid.

You may have noticed that I haven't mentioned the obvious source of entertainment for policemen – policewomen. I knew a lot ranging from one who was so naïve that she once actually said, 'Yes but what is a gang bang Sarge' to another who was very well endowed, expected everyone to have a quick grope as they passed and only got annoyed if their hands were dirty enough to leave finger marks on the front of her clean white blouse for her husband to see (he probably wouldn't have noticed as he was too busy with other ladies anyway!) Some of the lads got involved but I found policewomen generally to be a pretty (and often not very pretty) boring lot. There was a lady traffic warden called Rosemary though that I played games with regularly during our lunch breaks in Milford Haven – unfortunately it was only darts.

One Christmas Eve, a WRAF Corporal full of festive spirit came up to me in a busy shopping street. She said, 'My name's Carol', removed my helmet and placed it on the bonnet of a parked car, deftly placed my right hand inside her blouse and after giving me a kiss that seemed to last for at least five minutes, gently replaced my helmet and disappeared into the crowds. I had never seen her before and regrettably have never seen her since. It was just a bit embarrassing and got me a few ironic cheers from onlookers but it was very, very nice and certainly the most memorable of all the Christmas Carols.

Duty over Christmas was a fact of life. Normally we worked either Christmas Day or Boxing Day and to have both off was a very rare luxury. Christmas was either very busy with a succession of traffic accidents, thefts, drunks, sudden deaths and most commonly, domestic disputes or was very quiet with plenty of opportunities to relax. There never seemed to be a happy medium (except perhaps at the spiritualists Christmas party) but it is the relaxing ones you tend to remember. It was I think in 1974 when I was on early shift on Christmas Day. Apart from the problem of forcing your legs out of bed just a couple of hours after the Christmas Eve party, this was the favourite shift. You finished at 2pm before most of the trouble had started and had the rest of the holiday to look forward to. These were the days when Christmas lasted just two or three days not the two weeks or more it seems to now.

Sergeant Charlie Morris had invited me to join him on some 'house calls'. We finally set off at about ten thirty after an anxious wait when it seemed that Chief Inspector Brian Bebb would never go home (What the hell was he doing there on Christmas Day? we wondered). Charlie had a great nose for a free drink and by one-o-clock we had put away more than a few pints. At this point we arrived at the home of PC Dai Williams in Hakin who offered us a sample of his famous – or infamous home-brew. It came in three varieties – 'boy's', 'strong' and 'numb face'. We of course opted for 'numb face'.

After copious samples and a visit to Milford Rugby Club to round the morning off, we decided that we had better get back or I would be late going off duty and Charlie would be late for his dinner. I was driving the *Landrover* that they had given us to visit muddy refinery construction sites about six months after all the work there was finished and that was now being used as a totally unsuitable general purpose vehicle. I had got to Hamilton Terrace (Milford's 'sea front' road) when Charlie stopped singing, opened the sliding window, carefully removed his false teeth and placed them inside his helmet on his lap and after muttering, 'Don't stop, keep driving', proceeded to throw up along the whole length of the street and the whole side of the *Landrover*. Fortunately we only passed one startled old lady walking her dog and she probably thought that she was seeing things.

Charlie was on duty until 5pm and having recovered slightly he drove himself the three miles or so to his home at Johnston for his belated Christmas dinner. I heard later that he'd been gone at least fifteen minutes when there was a call from his wife asking, 'Where's Charlie?' She was told he was on his way and not to worry because an incident had delayed him. A search party was then urgently sent out to follow Charlie's route. No mangled wreckage was found and when they got to Johnston they saw Charlie's car neatly parked on his drive. It was a bit surprising therefore when another call came in from Mrs Morris demanding, 'Where the hell is Charlie, his dinner's ruined?' She eventually started a search and found Charlie fast asleep in bed, in full uniform including raincoat and boots with his helmet (still containing his false teeth) lying on his chest and all thoughts of dinner – and the rest of his shift blissfully forgotten.

Mum and Dad were visiting and Christmas lunch had been arranged for the whole family with Jennifer who by then was in residence at the Castle in St Ishmaels. For some reason I can't remember, I had gone to work in Jennifer's car, a green

Vauxhall Viva. I drove back to St Ishmaels and started to tuck into my turkey. I had only just started when my liquid consumption demanded a visit to the loo. At the Castle, you had to go through a couple of bedrooms to get to the bathroom and on the way back one of the beds looked particularly inviting. Two or three hours later I came to with absolutely no feeling in my face – you could have stuck pins in my cheeks and I wouldn't have felt a thing. I should have believed Dai Williams, 'numb face' it really was. The rest of my dinner tasted really good warmed up at teatime and I had enjoyed a great Christmas Day. Jennifer was not quite so happy though when a couple of weeks later she was in town with her car and an irate motorist accused her of forcing him off the road at the bottom of Herbrandston Hill at Christmas!

11: *THE LAST STRAW*

I had enjoyed my time as an Aide to CID – for one thing there was never any need to worry about being in uniform when you fancied a pint. I also discovered some new venues such as the bar at the Royal Navy Mine Depot just outside Milford. It had two full sized snooker tables and being classified as a 'Ministry of Defence Canteen' under the licensing laws it had two very major advantages. It was illegal for it to make a profit so the prices were ridiculously cheap and its opening hours were fixed by the Commanding Officer, who if he was present could change them according to how the evening developed. As you could imagine this gave scope for some memorable sessions.

The attachment also meant taking part in undercover operations as a 'new face' that wouldn't be known to criminals. The operations didn't always go as planned. CID chiefs suspected a house was being used for fairly major drugs dealing, information was received that a shipment was due at a certain time and a major observation plan was set up. A special vehicle was borrowed from the Regional Crime Squad and I was given the important job of driver. The vehicle was a battered old greengrocers van that appeared through the back windows to be stacked up with boxes of oranges and other fruit but actually contained a fully equipped observation post for three detectives. The plan was that I should drive to the appointed spot, pretend to break down and after spending a few minutes under the bonnet appear to give up and go for assistance leaving the van in place for the stakeout.

I drove for several miles and with a series of coughs, splutters and back-fires, the engine stopped. I spent about five minutes under the bonnet and climbed back into the cab to hear the voice of the Detective Sergeant through the communication tube saying, 'That was a great performance lad but we're in the wrong bloody place'. I then had the delicate task of telling him that we really had broken down. We eventually got the thing going only to break down twice more before arriving at the pre-arranged spot almost an hour late. I did my under the bonnet routine perfectly having had so many rehearsals and kicked the van with genuine feeling before wandering off. I hitched a lift back to Headquarters for a late meal break leaving three very dejected detectives in the back of the van. They were eventually towed back home and a few weeks later a similar operation was successful and several arrests were made. Needless to say the report made no mention of the original fiasco.

I was really pleased therefore when towards the end of 1974 I was told that I had been selected to attend an Initial CID Course at Bristol. The course was held at an old country mansion Kings Weston House on the outskirts of the city and was most enjoyable. Most of those on the course were found 'digs' in private houses but four of us were told that we had been 'unlucky' and would have to be accommodated in a small hotel just off Whiteladies Road near the BBC. We soon discovered that our bad luck meant that for ten weeks we would have to share good food and good accommodation with four chorus girls rehearsing and then performing in a show at the Bristol Hippodrome in a very nice little hotel with its own bar tucked away in the cellar and an owner willing to tell theatrical stories and serve beer into the small hours.

My enduring memory is of getting back from Kings Weston and whiling away the time before dinner by watching television. The dancing girls occupied the three piece suite and we would sit on the floor in front using their legs as backrests and occasionally having a shapely thigh draped over our shoulder as we watched *Captain Pugwash* before the Six o clock News. The course involved such hardships as watching porn for a couple of afternoons so that we would know the difference between illegal 'hard' and legal 'soft' and of course learning about the appearance (and effects!) of controlled drugs such as cannabis, amphetamines and heroin (speed was very new and crack didn't even exist then). We had regular visiting speakers including a former prison governor, a pathologist, a forensic scientist and a Scotland Yard Murder Squad detective who spent most of the day taking the piss out of and totally winding up the Welsh contingent with continuous references to sheep and grandmothers – one actually walked out but got no sympathy and a real rollicking from the instructors for 'folding under pressure'.

One day we were told we were being given an observation test. We were all taken to a basement room containing a very large table literally covered in dozens of different items. We were told we had ten minutes before we would be taken back to the classroom and tested on what we had seen. We were about half way through peering at the table trying to memorise exactly what was there and what was next to what when I caught a movement out of the corner of my eye. A man and a woman had come into the room through one door and were passing through to go out through another. The girl was very attractive and my eyes stayed with her until the couple left the room and I dragged my attention back to the table. In the classroom the test began and every single question was about the couple that had briefly strolled through and the contents of the table weren't even mentioned. Some of the lads hadn't even seen them they were so concerned with staring at the table and scored nil. I scored well, especially on the questions about the girl's appearance and clothes. There's obviously a lot to be said for a wandering eye.

The last week of the course was something special. The whole week was shown on the programme as 'Murder Investigation'. We were split up into small teams and had to investigate a 'murder' that had taken place and interview numbers of off-duty Bristol City policemen who played the parts of witnesses and suspects and were expert at spreading total confusion. On the first day one of the lads on the course went missing at lunchtime and we were told that he had been rushed to Bristol Royal Infirmary and was too seriously ill for visitors. On the second day one of the most popular lads on the course lost his cool during a vicious de-briefing, swore at the chief instructor and was thrown off the course to be sent back to his home force in disgrace. By the end of that day every group had arrested 'the wrong man' at least once and the task seemed absolutely hopeless – how the hell would we get through three more days of this? At coffee break on the third day all was revealed. Our 'seriously ill' and 'disgraced' colleagues both strolled back in having spent the time hiding down at Bristol's Bridewell police station and we were told that with the information we had been given we could never have identified the murderer. It was all a set up to see how well we coped with pressure. We were sworn to secrecy as far as any future course members were concerned and having been through it we happily agreed. But I've told you all now.

We spent one happy day with the Army at Chepstow watching things being blown up and shot at and enduring one lecture where a maniac SAS Sergeant spent the whole hour detonating every so often, small charges that he had placed on our chairs and tables and ones that we set off ourselves by treading on mats or opening books that he had given us to look at. Nothing was big enough to hurt but was loud enough to make you check your underpants. As part of the day's entertainment the Army showed us a selection of their latest small arms and let us have a go with them on an outside range. The idiot next to me was firing a semi-automatic rifle and had been told by the instructor to keep it on single shot. Naturally being a copper and being Welsh he switched it to rapid fire. He hadn't a clue as to how to control the gun when it started bucking and twirling about spraying live bullets everywhere in wild arcs. I may have imagined it but I thought I felt the wind of some of them before he finally realised that all he had to do was take his finger off the bloody trigger. The Army were not amused.

During my service I managed to avoid looking down the barrel of a gun (apart from at Chepstow!) and only ever fired a weapon two or three times at a target – if you don't count targets covered in fur or feathers. There was very little operational use of firearms in my day but we still had a few authorised users who were specially selected and trained. At Milford the powers that be had obviously spent many hours sifting through personal files to find men of intelligence, integrity, coolness and professionalism but had then decided that it was a lot easier to pick the only two that had ever been in the Army. It was my opinion then that anyone silly enough to join the Army should never be allowed near a gun anyway and these two fully justified that view. In any shoot out I would have felt far safer standing next to the criminal than alongside either of them.

One was Ron Jones who shared his name with the Chief Constable, appeared to be as thick as the proverbial two short planks but during his Army days had learned a lot of native cunning and was a past master at avoiding any situation likely to involve work. In any siege situation we would probably have spent the first hour looking for him. The other 'specialist' was

Paddy Loam, a likeable lad but accident-prone. If twenty drunks were arrested in a month he would get the only one to turn violent. If we arrested ten burglars he would invariably get the only one to resist arrest and then complain that he had been subjected to police brutality. If we dealt with a hundred road traffic accidents Paddy would get the only one between someone with diplomatic immunity and a non-English speaking illegal immigrant in a stolen car. When the suspension collapsed and the front wheels fell off our *Austin 1100* area car (that's when we got the *Landrover*), you've guessed it - Paddy was driving. Thankfully we never had to call on the services of either of them.

I often wondered what my reaction would have been if I had been faced with a gun. I knew two men who had received bravery awards for disarming and arresting dangerous criminals and both said that the thought of being killed or injured never entered their heads. It wasn't until after it was all over that the shakes set in. Possibly faced with the same situation I would have acted in the same way or perhaps I would have asked the old question, 'What do you call a Irishman with a machine gun?' and very quickly come up with the answer, 'Sir'. I shall never know but I suppose I should be grateful that I was never forced to find out.

I finished the CID Course in December 1974 with an overall average of 78% in my final examinations and third place out of thirty on the course. I was happy with a very favourable assessment that concluded by saying, 'altogether a valuable member of the course, he was popular with fellow students and staff alike'. I knew that there would be a vacancy for a Detective Constable at Milford Haven in the New year and I knew that I couldn't have done more to earn it. As we moved into 1975 I was not a happy bunny when I discovered that the vacancy had gone to a man whose position on the course had been down in the twenties and that it was almost certain that he had been told that he had got the job before we even took the final exams. It was at that point that I began to wonder whether Dyfed Powys Police should possibly stick their job where the sun didn't shine. Looking back, it was the beginning of the end.

Dad took slightly early retirement from *AC Delco* on 31 January 1975 and after receiving an offer for *The Hyde* from the council that had tried and failed to compulsorily purchase it many years before, he and Mum decided to move to Pembrokeshire. A deal was done for them to move to a bungalow to be built for them by Graham Sutton at 5 Brookside, St Ishmaels. At the time my brother Nigel was still living at home and having completed an apprenticeship was working at the same company as my father. He had a good job, no idea whether he could get a similar one in Pembrokeshire and a good circle of friends. He weighed up the pros and cons and finally, like any good engineer, made a decision based on pure science – he tossed a coin. It came down Pembrokeshire and it worked out well. He soon found himself a very good job with a company based on the Thornton Industrial Estate and several years later found himself a Pembrokeshire wife.

One of the benefits of living in Dale was the small village shop run by Margaret Fisher, wife of Stewart Fisher who had installed our new windows when we moved in. Apart from topping up with odd bits of shopping and buying the cigarettes I smoked in those days its greatest available service was that purchases could be 'put on the book' to be settled when the next pay cheque came in. This was a great asset then as times were a bit hard with mortgage interest rates forever rising. One month when I went in to settle my bill, it seemed a bit high and so unusually, I asked to have a look at the actual book. Yes, there were two packets of fags closer together than would be normal and the clincher, a box of matches. I never bought matches and always used a lighter. The police continued their enquiries and it transpired that a certain son and a certain niece who shall both be nameless had booked them down to me and had hidden them in the storm drain which ran under the road onto Dale beach and which was their little private smoking room. They were let off with a caution.

Mention of Stewart Fisher reminds me of when I decided to *Snowcem* our new abode. I did the back walls without a problem. The front was the same height above the ground but with the garden sloping down to the road, it seemed much higher but I just about managed. Finally, I came to the gable end and my ladders just wouldn't reach to the top so I asked Stewart if he had a set I could borrow. I expected a nice solid wood or metal extender but he arrived with a single piece ladder plenty high enough but with more bounce than a trampoline. Stewart watched me climb about half way up, hanging on for dear life, before he laughed and said, 'Come on down, I'll do it' This he did in no time at all, brush in one hand, large tin of *Snowcem* in the other actually using the bounce to reach further. I was so grateful.

1975 passed without a great deal to remember. In April Charlie Morris was promoted to Inspector and moved to Llanelli – a whole new way of life for him and also for those of us who had shared his regular pub visits in Milford. At Charlie's leaving party a speech was made by one of our senior PCs Bill Lennon. Afterwards, Charlie said, 'Bill did that very well but I wasn't sure whether he was saying farewell, making a political speech or giving me a bollocking'. I spent another pleasurable summer riding my motorbike from beach to beach, enjoying the sights and doing as little as possible. In October I went to the Vale

Garage at Neyland where I bought a *Simca 1500* JDE 554L for £1150 and got an incredible £700 part exchange on the *Toledo* that had required chicken wire, old baked bean tins and pounds of filler to cover all the rust holes.

By now we were very much part of the community in Dale. I particularly remember Haidee playing *Angela* in *Cinderella Revisited* the WI pantomime and Doug playing *Bay-leaf the Gardener* in the school concert both in the village's Coronation Hall and in 1974 I turned my wheelbarrow into a pink *Court Lines* (gone bust a few days before) aircraft for the village carnival with Douglas pushing it as the pilot. Bill was dressed as a Frenchman with beret in a dumper truck, celebrating or perhaps expressing horror at the thought of the proposed Channel Tunnel or maybe something to do with what we then called the Common Market.

Dale Carnival – Bill on the dumper truck in the 'French' beret & Douglas piloting his pink wheelbarrow airliner

I was voted on to the Coronation Hall Committee and eventually became Chairman. I was arm-twisted onto the village Carnival Committee and became Treasurer then Chairman and later I would be very much involved in the village's Silver Jubilee celebrations in 1977. All this helped our integration into the village as It gave me contact with people I would not normally have met on duty or in the pub. Names that still come to mind are Mr & Mrs Bill Copestake, Nigel Collis, Audrey Hobbs, Diane Davies, Mil Reynolds, Bob Medway, Mary Brand and Celia John.I was also for a time the village's milkman! Sid Brooks who ran the two-pump petrol station on the sea front and also the local milk round had a heart attack – certainly not through overwork. On the milk round all Sid did was drive the van; it was his wife Iris who ran up and down all the steps with the bottles. On the pumps he spent hours sitting in his little wooden hut waiting for the next customer but in the summer would be endlessly running out and telling holidaymakers, 'You can't park here, this is a filling station'. I used to call it the 'THISISA' filling station. Once there was an event on at the Coronation Hall and I saw Iris staggering in with a heavy water urn and Sid strolling along behind carrying just two pints of milk. She even spent part of every evening rolling cigarettes to fill Sid's tin for the following day. Anyway Sid had his heart attack and Iris couldn't drive so a group of us including one of the Trinity House lighthouse men from St Anne's Head and Paul Backhouse one of HM Coastguards who was ex-Metropolitan Police River Patrol and who, some years later would become landlord at the Griffin Inn, took turns to drive when we were off duty so that Iris always had a driver until Sid was fit again.

Cinderella Re-visited: **Haidee front left. Also in the picture are Paddy Tamsett, Celia John, Cllr. Bertie Edwards, June Emerson, Connie Hazell, Enid Davies and Edie Gilpin**

It didn't take long each day because unlike Sid, we did our share of bottle rattling as well as driving. I shall always remember my first visit to Dale Fort with the milk van. We had to deliver a small churn there and carry it into the kitchens. I picked it up and Iris protested, 'I usually do that'. It weighed a ton! I thoroughly enjoyed the experience, even when it meant getting wet and I remember one morning up at St Anne's Head when I had to turn the van round before I could get out because the wind was blowing too strongly for me to open the door against it. Sid eventually was allowed to drive and came back to work and whether it was because his stand-ins shamed him or whether his doctor insisted, he actually started to get off his backside and deliver a few bottles of milk.

At around this time Malcolm Rowlands started talking about leaving the Brook Inn at St Ishmaels and the thought of us taking over was quite appealing. It wasn't to be (not that time anyway) because when Malcolm finally moved to Weston-Super-Mare it was the total and complete lunatic George Dodd who took over. George became legendary within a few months and people used to come for miles just to see him being rude to customers. I saw him once hand menus to an elderly couple. They studied them for a while and one very quietly remarked, 'It's a little expensive my dear' with which George grabbed the menus from them and shouted, 'If you want the f***ing Salvation Army, try f***ing Milford'. The menu was often supplemented by chalked messages on the beams such as 'Fresh Mackerel. Caught Today' (caught straight from the freezer some months after the mackerel season had ended).

He once insisted that someone who had fainted be dragged outside immediately because, 'If they bloody die in here it's bad for trade'. He had been having problems with the juke box and when it went wrong again, he picked it up bodily and threw it out into the road outside before phoning the company and telling them where they could collect it from. He chased one regular from the premises with a Samurai sword and often banned customers for the flimsiest of reasons – Bill Roberts, headmaster at the village school, was once briefly banned for 'being a teacher' but in fairness he wasn't singled out as Dodd had decided to bar all teachers.

Malcolm Rowlands had become a good friend since I moved to Pembrokeshire. I was a frequent visitor to the *Brook* both on and off duty and when my parents were visiting it was our pub of choice. During the winter months, if I was working a 2-10pm shift in Milford, I would rush away to get to St Ishmaels before 'shut tap' and even if I had no cash in my pocket, my credit was always good with Malcolm for a quick pint or so. He moved to Weston-Super-Mare when he left and some time later, it was probably when I was on my CID course in Bristol because I was on my own, he invited me to visit. His 'local' was the Conservative Club and he introduced me to a drink I had never tried before and never have since. This was a double whisky in a fairly large spirit glass topped up with milk chilled in the fridge before the pint bottle was brought to our table. I totally lost count of how many we consumed but I know we got through more than one bottle of milk. Next morning I woke expecting a well deserved hangover but had a totally clear head, a well settled stomach and after a hearty breakfast drove back to Pembrokeshire with no trouble at all.

The possibility of taking the Brook had however prompted me to invoke Police Regulations and demand my right to a meeting with the Chief Constable, who by now was R B Thomas, to discuss my future. Basically I wanted to see if there was any chance of promotion before I made any career decision. I knew that he couldn't say that I would be promoted in the near future but I suggested that he should be able to tell me if I didn't have a snowball's chance in Hell. He wouldn't even commit himself to that. It was like talking to a ball of cotton wool. I took the opportunity to ask why I hadn't been given the CID job and he said I was obviously better qualified but I would have needed to live in Milford to do the job and I had got my own house in Dale. I told him in no uncertain terms that it would have been nice to be asked whether I would have been willing to move. He seemed quite impressed that I wasn't frightened and was willing to have a go at him. He didn't get stroppy about it as some senior officers certainly would have done and I shall never know whether I improved my promotion prospects or totally wrote them off.

During my time as village bobby (seasonal) on the Dale beat there were two major happenings both at Marloes, both big enough to make the national press but strangely enough, neither of which I had anything whatsoever to do with. The first was centred around the Lobster Pot when their pools syndicate had a major win. For nine years a syndicate had been entering the same numbers on the *Treble Chance* without success but eventually the coupon filled in by landlord Dennis Blackman came up with £41,108 for the 34 members of the syndicate - £1209 each with some families having more than one share. Needless to say, celebrations were virtually endless with Dennis probably taking very nearly as much over the bar as he had won. I very tactfully thought it best to avoid Marloes for a week or so until the celebrations and hangovers had subsided. Two people who had left the syndicate not long before the win were said by the press to have, 'taken it philosophically'. I bet they did!

The second occurrence involved someone who had featured in the pools win celebration press photos and who for no apparent reason suddenly stabbed his wife to death in their home. I was not on duty at the time and a 999 call had resulted in his almost immediate arrest when driving out of Pembrokeshire on the A40. I was excluded from all subsequent enquiries because the man, who I won't name, had been known to me almost as long as I had known Pembrokeshire and was a fellow member of the *Lobster Pot* darts team. On reflection, he had never been quite 'one of the boys' and was someone that you felt you never really fully got to know. I did manage to get a sneaky look at a copy of the case file 'accidentally' left out when I was in Milford police station. The most interesting part was the psychiatric report which revealed that he had been killing chickens and small animals since he was a child and that stabbing his wife had probably given him the biggest sexual 'high' of his life.

Early in 1976 I was back in Milford Haven again and started getting a lot of stomach pain. The doctor told me it was a duodenal ulcer and signed me off sick. Years later I discovered the problem was in fact a hiatus hernia and I had been misdiagnosed but the treatment would have been very much the same anyway. The doctor obviously thought that the 'ulcer' was stress related and each time I saw him he asked, 'Do you feel like going back to work yet?' and with the prospect of working in Milford in the wet and the cold, every time I quite truthfully answered, 'No'. The result was that I was off work for some considerable time.

A couple of mates popped in now and then to see if I was still alive but not once did I get a visit from 'management' i.e. a Sergeant or an Inspector. Being 'on the sick', Mum and Dad now being in residence in St Ishmaels and the Cleddau Bridge now having opened gave opportunities to explore the South of the County and the delights of Angle, Bosheston, Freshwater East, Manorbier, Amroth and Lydstep Haven and discovering that the likes of Saundersfoot and Tenby were very much best sampled 'out of season'. I enjoyed visiting Pembroke itself and found it very interesting – perhaps foreseeing the future.

Landlord Mr. Dennis Blackman pours the drinks for his pools syndicate outside the Lobster Pot at Marloes last night.

Villagers set to celebrate big pools win they all share

By JIM SMITH

LANDLORD DENNIS Blackman was the toast of the Pembrokeshire village of Marloes last night after he landed a pools win shared by almost every household.

Mr. Blackman, of the Lobster Pot Inn, is one of a syndicate of 34 villagers who are believed to have won about £50,000 with two first dividends on Littlewoods.

Virtually every household in the village of 288 people is likely to benefit from the win, whic hwill be officially known today.

The syndicate, made up of farmworkers, refinery men and other workmen, did not know of their big win until a pools representative called at the local on Monday.

It was while I was still off sick that I received a phone call out of the blue from the Inspector at Milford. He told me that Dale would be closed as a rural beat and would no longer be operated in the summer months. I would work full time in Milford and someone would come tomorrow to collect all my books and papers. That was it. No warning, no consultation. Although other rural stations were also being closed it was still like a thump in the guts. The next day as promised, two lads from Milford came out to collect all the paperwork. In a final act of defiance I gave them an out of date Beat Book and kept the up to date one (which contained every bit of information and intelligence I had gathered on the area). But as everything was taken away it was like seeing my life disappearing in two cardboard boxes. After they had gone I went up to the top of my garden under the trees and I'm not ashamed to say that I cried. That was it. That was the last straw. F*** the police force and everybody in it.

I saw a job advertised in the *Western Telegraph* – not a chance, Welsh speaking an advantage, but I was so pissed off I applied anyway. I was surprised therefore to be called to an interview at the Royal Ivy Bush Hotel in Carmarthen on 27 May 1976 and even more surprised to be offered the job for which I discovered later there had been over fifty applicants. It meant a big drop in pay - £3,555 to £2,691 but Haidee was working at the DHSS in Haverfordwest by then so it didn't need a lot of thought. I typed my letter of resignation the following day – nearly two pages of close typed foolscap stressing my fundamental disagreement with the new rural policing policy, the loss of 'status' posts such as traffic, admin and rural beats for senior Constables and the failure of senior officers to apply even basic man management principles including sick visits! – someone may have read it. I worked my notice enjoying saying exactly what I thought to everyone who deserved it and totally flouting Police Regulations by working behind the bar at St Ishmaels Sports and Social Club on my evenings off. My last day of duty was 30 June and my new job started the following day.

If you asked me whether if I had my time again I would still join the police force, I would probably say 'No' and certainly say 'No' as things are in the job today. Even back then the hassle, the bad management and the restrictions on social life were all so much part of the job that you didn't really realise how bad they were until you left. It was like the man who kept hitting himself on the head with a hammer because it was lovely when he stopped. On the other hand it was an experience I wouldn't have missed for the world. The contrasts and variations from day to day made it like no other job could possibly be. In the same week I had enjoyed a bottle of beer with a millionaire Lord of the Realm in his kitchen and shared a pot of thick black tea with a tramp at his roadside camp fire on the A1 in Huntingdonshire.

I had met and chatted with prominent politicians of the day such as Enoch Powell and Richard Marsh in Cambridge and made Barbara Castle's driver (she was the only Minister of Transport who couldn't drive) move her car when she came to speak in Marloes village hall. I had been bought drinks by European Heavyweight Champion Joe Bugner and arrested a former British Champion for burglary. I had fed an MP's cat while he was away on holiday and pinched apples from his garden when he was home. I had been given a cigar by Jimmy Savile (before anyone had any doubts about him), taken a bedside statement from Allan Clarke the lead singer of *The Hollies* in Huntingdon Hospital and had a drink with a lesser showbiz star as she strolled topless round her dressing room at Milford Haven Football Club at Marble Hall (with my young companion fresh from the Cardiganshire hills with eyes like saucers and totally speechless). In the Griffin at Dale I had talked boats with transatlantic yachtswoman Nicolette Milnes-Walker and talked birds with former TV newsreader Robert Dougal. Also in Dale I had chatted to actress Hilda Braid (Wolfie's Mum in *Citizen Smith*) who had a holiday home at The Hooskses on the old airfield. I had worked alongside former World's Strongest Man Geoff Capes, shaken hands with the Duke of Edinburgh and been spat on by Young Socialist Workers. Among the aggro and often the boredom there was a lot to enjoy.

12: *WITH THE HERALD BARD*

My new employer was Dyfed Rural Council. On April Fool's Day 1974, the Government in all its wisdom had amalgamated Pembrokeshire, Carmarthenshire and Cardiganshire County Councils and called the resulting monster Dyfed County Council. It also messed about with District Councils leaving Pembrokeshire with just two – Preseli and South Pembrokeshire. At the same time it decided that (only in Wales and not in England!), Parish Councils should be called Community Councils. Community Councils were given the power to resolve to call themselves Town Council and to call their Chairman Town Mayor. In 1996 the Government eventually saw sense and disbanded Dyfed. None of this had anything to do with Dyfed Rural Council.

Before all this happened, bodies called Community Councils had been formed in Pembrokeshire, Cardiganshire and Carmarthenshire as far back as the 1930's with the purpose of assisting and making more effective local charities and voluntary organisations, acting as a forum for Parish Councils and encouraging music, drama and rural crafts. With the advent of Dyfed, the three had decided to amalgamate but retained offices in Haverfordwest, Carmarthen and Aberaeron with the Director based in Haverfordwest. The Pembrokeshire Community Council had had involvement over the years with the Rural Industries Committee, the Local History Society, the Guild of Craftsmen, Meals on Wheels and the West Wales Tourism Committee but by the time I arrived the three main activities were providing a secretariat for the Dyfed Association of Local (Town & Community) Councils, giving advice to these Councils and acting as a link between them and the National

Association of Local Councils, advising and assisting Village Hall Committees and providing a secretariat and advice for local Old Peoples Welfare Committees (The forerunners of Age Concern).

My new job sounded very grand and the title and brief description was: 'Administrative Officer reporting to the Director and to take full charge of the Haverfordwest office in his absence'. When he was away, which was frequently, the office of which I took full charge normally comprised a receptionist/typist and me! The Director was Dillwyn Miles. I had first heard his name when I was Chairman of the Dale Village Hall Committee and our Secretary Connie Hazel, somewhat unhappy with the advice she had received, had said something like, 'It's all right for Dillwyn Miles sitting up in his ivory tower in Haverfordwest'. I now knew that the 'ivory tower' was in fact a very tatty first floor office in Victoria Place at the bottom of High Street but I was soon to learn that Dillwyn Miles was an extraordinary man.

William James Dillwyn Miles was born in Newport, Pembrokeshire in 1915 and was a fairly well-worn sixty years of age when I first went to work with him. When his father died, he was attending Fishguard High School and a few weeks later passed his School Board Certificate. Following this success he received a visit from a number of members of Newport Parish Council and Burial Board who invited him to become their Clerk at a salary of £10 per annum. The vacancy was due to the previous Clerk embezzling funds and as a result Dillwyn became at sixteen years of age the youngest ever Clerk to a Parish Council anywhere in England and Wales.

He stayed in post until leaving for the University of Wales, Aberystwyth in 1935 at which point, in recognition of his services, he was appointed a Burgess of the Town & Corporation of Newport (While still under-age to have been a Councillor). Later he was elected a councillor and became Mayor of Newport on four occasions between 1950 and 1980. After leaving university he held several teaching posts in Pembrokeshire until the outbreak of war in 1939 when he enlisted in the Royal Army Service Corps. He served mostly in Palestine but following the invasion of Syria and the surrender of its forces he had the job of drafting and typing the lengthy peace agreement and later newspaper reports of the armistice mentioned the excellent services of the 'young Welsh poet'. After the war he worked in London for two years at Palestine House but returned to Pembrokeshire and Newport and was an external lecturer for the University of Wales, then Community Centres Officer for Wales before in 1954 becoming General Secretary and then Director of the Pembrokeshire Rural Community Council which was to become Dyfed Rural Council.

His achievements and posts held are endless and I have probably forgotten more than a few. He was a member of the Gorsedd of Bards of the Welsh National Eisteddfod holding the posts of both Grand Sword Bearer and Herald Bard taking part in the investiture of the Prince of Wales. He served on the Council of the National Eisteddfod of Wales, the National Playing Fields Association, the National Library of Wales, the Court of Governors of the University of Wales, the Mental Health Review Tribunal for Wales, the Nature Conservancy for Wales, the Prince of Wales Committee for Wales and was Chairman of the National Association of Local Councils.

In Pembrokeshire he was a member of Haverfordwest Borough Council becoming Mayor of Haverfordwest and Admiral of the Port, Sheriff of the Town & County of Haverfordwest, member of the Pembrokeshire Coast National Park Committee, Secretary of the West Wales Field Society which became the West Wales Wildlife Trust and as such he was very much involved in the acquisition of Skomer Island as a nature reserve. He revived the Pembrokeshire Local History Society and edited the *Pembrokeshire Historian* for about thirty years. He edited *Nature in Wales* and founded the Association of Trusts for the Nature Conservation in Wales. He wrote more than twenty books including *The Castles of Pembrokeshire, The Pembrokeshire Coast National Park, The Sheriffs of the County of Pembroke, The Secrets of The Bards of Britain* and *A Pembrokeshire Anthology.*

Quite a list of achievements (with almost certainly many missing) but they all pale into insignificance with something he told me one day. He was a personal friend of Fiona Richmond !!! Fiona (real name Julia Harrison and a genuine vicar's daughter) was a *Bunny Girl* then for seven years was the girlfriend of Paul Raymond the 'King of Soho' who owned strip clubs and 'top shelf' magazines in the 1970's. She appeared in X-rated films such as *Expose, Hard Core* and *Let's Get Laid* and very often appeared nude and wrote sexy articles in the magazines published by Raymond. He bought her a yellow E-type Jaguar with the registration plate FU 2 but grabbed it back the day after they split up. I was a bit dubious about Dillwyn's claim at the time but I should have known better. One day I was investigating a very dusty storeroom when I found alongside stacks of back numbers of *Pembrokeshire Historian* and *Nature in Wales,* similar stacks of *Men Only* and *Razzle* complete with

little notes indicating that they were indeed complimentary copies from the gorgeous girl herself. Now in her seventies, she is living with her second husband in Grenada and sculpts driftwood. Dillwyn died in August 2007 aged 91.

Working with Dillwyn was quite an experience and rarely a problem as he would usually tell you exactly what he wanted and then let you get on with it but with all his many interests it was often hard to tell whether you were actually working for Dyfed Rural Council or for him. Sometimes however it was quite obvious – I was asked once to address a large number of envelopes to members of the Gorsedd of Bards by hand in Welsh. I have no idea why he wanted them handwritten but did say that he didn't trust our typist to copy the Welsh. So I can just about claim to have been Deputy Herald Bard.

Dillwyn the Bard

The only time I saw Dillwyn just ever so slightly annoyed was when fairly early on in my time there he asked me to send out an advice circular to all our Old Peoples Welfare Committees. This I did during one of his many absences from the office and when he got back he had a look at my work and told me quietly but very firmly that I shouldn't have signed it and that everything leaving the office should go out in his name. Then after a lengthy pause he said, 'But it was very well written'.

Much of my work was liaising with and advising Old Peoples Welfare Committees, sometimes speaking at evening meetings often in remote village halls in parts of Pembrokeshire I hadn't visited before. Most of the rest of the time I was dealing with Clerks to Parish Councils who were seeking advice or guidance. Sometimes I would need to consult the National Association in London but less frequently as I became very familiar with what was then our 'bible', The Local Government Act 1972. I had first became interested in local government when my mother was for a number of years a Parish Councillor in our home village and when the (very) part-time post of Clerk to Marloes Community Council became vacant in January 1976, I felt I could easily fit it in with my full-time job and that I now had the knowledge and confidence to apply. That confidence grew when I attended for interview and found that the chairman of the panel was the first Pembrokeshire man that I had ever met – Cllr. Bobby Morgan of East Hook Farm. I got the job.

During the time that I was doing the occasional stint behind the bar at St Ishmaels Sports and Social Club, I set off from Dale in my *Simca 1500* one very wet evening to go and pull a few pints. Driving round the village's one-way system, I had passed the road to St Annes Head and the cemetery when I saw a large puddle of water. A very small stream passed under the road at this point but I had never seen standing water there before so I made the mistake of ploughing straight in. The rubber gaiter around my gear lever had a split in it and immediately a fountain of water gushed up through the split powerful enough to widen it and to hit the roof of the car soaking me and everything inside. I managed to keep going to 'Tish', dried out a bit and finished my shift. Needless to say, the car wouldn't start and I had to get a lift home and arrange for Bill Collett of Sunnyside Garage, St Ishmaels to sort out the car and get it back to me the following day. Then came the task of removing and drying out all the carpets. This went very well until I put them back and found that they had shrunk and I now had a couple of inches of bare metal all around them when fitted

Not being able to afford a change, I still had the *Simca* when working for Dillwyn and when he asked me to attend a meeting in Carmarthen on his behalf – oh and by the way, would I be kind enough to transport three elderly female delegates, I had little choice. On the appointed day, I picked them up, I think one was from Milford and having got them all loaded aboard my green not at all mean machine, I set off along the A40. About half way to Carmarthen I had a rear tyre blow-out. I managed to get off the road safely and pulled into a farm entrance Wearing my best suit, I got the jack and spare wheel out of the boot. I unloaded two of my passengers who were no lightweights but decided to leave one, who was light, frail and who had taken ages to get in, where she was on the back seat. I started to jack the car up and had almost got the wheel off the ground when with a loud crack, the bodywork collapsed and the jack went through the jacking point. There was nothing I could do without a large trolley jack so I set off on the several hundred yard hike to the farm.

Arriving at the farm, there was no answer to my knock so I started looking around the barns to see if I could find a suitable jack when an old crone appeared from nowhere demanding to know what I was doing on her land. She eventually listened to the fact that I had not one but three elderly ladies in distress and went off to find her son. He came up with an ideal jack and very kindly accompanied me as I dragged the jack all the way to back to the car. I soon fitted the spare and found that the son had again very kindly buggered off leaving me to drag the jack all the way back to the barn. So dusty, dirty, sweaty, in my best suit and now late, I loaded the ladies up and set off again towards Carmarthen. On the outskirts of town suddenly there were blues and twos behind me and I was pulled over for speeding. Yet further delay but not a problem – or so I thought. In those good old days before automatic or civilian operated speed cameras, if you were stopped for speeding it was either after being followed for a certain distance or after being timed between two measured points. Letting it be known that you were 'Job' or 'Ex-Job' would always be enough for you to be sent on your way with a smile and at worst a warning. But not this time. I had had the misfortune to have been stopped by a young, keen, Welsh speaking, probably English hating, possibly covert member of Cymdeithas yr Iaith Gymraeg (rare in the Police but there were a few). All I could do was insist that he record my occupation 'Community Relations Administrative Officer' in full when I knew that the space on the form was only half an inch long. We got to the meeting, not too late but my passengers were very quiet on the way home. I wasn't so quiet when my £14 fine came through.

My tatty first-floor office came into its own on 23 June 1977 when the Queen visited Haverfordwest on her Silver Jubilee tour. Dillwyn had the day off – probably shaking the Queen's hand somewhere in one capacity or another so I was able to invite my wife Haidee in for a grandstand view. We had just that, an excellent panoramic view of the Queen's walkabout and when the next *Western Telegraph* appeared it featured a lovely photograph of Her Majesty with the pair of us hanging out of the window just above her head. I expected some sort of comment from Dillwyn but none was forthcoming.

So life went on, me commuting to Haverfordwest and Haidee by this time working in the retail side at Dale Sailing Company on the front at Dale. My job was OK but becoming routine and not very challenging and the prospects of advancement were virtually nil. Dyfed Rural Council was a very small organisation and if Dillwyn ever decided to retire then his deputy Daffyd M. Jones at Aberaeron would be certain to succeed him – a prophecy that proved correct some years later. I was just drifting along, not actively looking for anything else but knowing that I couldn't stay where I was. Then we heard that George Dodd was leaving the Brook Inn.

The Queen in Haverfordwest. We are leaning out of our window top centre of the picture.

13:   PUB LANDLORD

I wasn't a stranger to a place behind a bar. In one of the pubs in my home village we once had an arrangement whereby if the police visited when we were still there after time had been called, I would immediately transform from customer to staff, collecting and washing glasses while the rest of the family 'waited for me to finish work' so I could drive them home'. At times, I would actually pull a pint for the visiting Constable. When I was with the Meteorological Office in Bracknell and switched from shift work to days, I worked a couple of evenings a week at The Boot in Park Road to compensate for the loss of shift allowance. The Boot was only a short walk from the Met Office roundabout and was my usual watering hole when out with my mates. I served my 'apprenticeship' there learning how to pull a proper pint with a beer handle, pour a proper pint of the new fangled 'keg' beers such as *Whitbread Tankard* and all other aspects of bar work including the now dead art of adding up the price of a 'round' in your head.

As already mentioned, as soon as I started working out my notice after resigning from Dyfed Powys Police, I did a few shifts behind the bar at St Ishmaels Sports & Social Club and found that I still got pleasure from the work. I knew a good many of the members either through contact in my job as a copper or as darts league opponents and enjoyed my time there. The exception to this was Bingo Night when you would see customers, many of them women, who you never saw on any other night. Instead of a steady stream of orders there would be spells of inactivity behind the bar followed by desperate rushes between bingo sessions when I perfected the art of sarcasm and different ways of suggesting that little magic words like 'please' and 'thank you' could possibly get them served quicker next time. Once each rush was over, I would tidy up ready for the next one but always keep a few empty bottles back. Then, when total silence fell as the next call of 'House' approached, I would lob them one at a time into the bottle bin enjoying the glares and occasional shushes forthcoming. I had always hated bingo but I had discovered a way to almost enjoy it. I also discovered limited cellar skills such as changing kegs and Co2 gas cylinders.

So, I knew that I enjoyed (except for Bingo) serving behind a bar, I knew I had the ability to cope with the administrative and financial side of things, I knew that virtually all of my police work had involved dealing with people, I knew deep down that running a pub had really been an ambition for some time. We had actually made enquiries when we were at Sawtry and had heard that the landlord at the Robin Hood, my favourite pub in St Ives, was about to retire but that had come to nothing. There was however a hell of a lot to consider. Was it something that Haidee would want to do as she would be massively involved? How would it affect the boys who were then aged just fourteen and eleven? Was The Brook a viable proposition with St Ishmaels Sports & Social Club and The Copper Coins Club in the same small village and with The Lobster Pot and The Griffin nearby? Where would we find the considerable sum of money needed to take up the tenancy if our application was successful?

In the end, consideration didn't take too long. Most importantly, Haidee was willing to take on what would be a huge commitment and was, as ever, fully supportive of anything I decided to do. The boys both thought that living in a pub would be akin to being in paradise and we thought that we could keep them suitably insulated from any unwelcome influences. The

Sports & Social Club didn't serve food, the Copper Coins didn't open at lunchtimes and food would almost certainly be a major source of the Brook's income especially in the Summer. Add to this all the customers that George Dodd had barred being likely to want to come back, friends, family and acquaintances likely to want to become customers and the past trade levels I had myself witnessed over the years the financial viability seemed promising. Finally and most surprisingly, the same bank manager who often wrote to us about going a few pounds overdrawn at the end of a month when a regular salary cheque was coming in was quite happy to lend me thousands of pounds when nothing at all could be guaranteed.

The Brook was a James Williams house. The company, based in Narberth owned and supplied just over seventy pubs in West Wales, mostly in Pembrokeshire. Occupancy was on a quarterly tenancy basis and tenants were 'tied' so that virtually everything drinkable had to be purchased from James Williams but there was a free hand with all food and non alcoholic supplies such as (shock horror) cigarettes and tobacco. After even more thought, chats with family and friends – and the bank manager at *Lloyds*, we submitted our application, attended for interview in Narberth and were actually somewhat surprised when we were offered the tenancy. The agreement was drawn up on 7 July and we signed on the dotted line on 16 July but as I have said it was an old fashioned tenancy which was only changed on one of the four traditional quarter days of Lady Day (25 March), Mid-Summer (24 June), Michaelmas (29 September) and Christmas Day so we had to wait until Michaelmas with plenty of time to make all the necessary arrangements and plenty of time to wonder if we were doing the right thing.

St Ishmaels – The Brook Inn is almost dead centre opposite the bungalow with the C shaped lawn. Mum & Dad's bungalow is the right of the three below the irrigation pond. The Copper Coins Club is the flat roofed building far left.

The first decision we made was that we would keep 77 Blue Anchor Way, probably turning it into a Summer let as many of the houses in the road already were. This would give us an escape route if things didn't turn out right but also meant that we would be paying off a mortgage as well as rent for the Brook. The rent was set at £500 a year payable quarterly in arrears but rising to £800 from 26 December 1981. I submitted my resignation to Dillwyn Miles as did Haidee to Dale Sailing Company but we both kept working pretty much up to the day we would take over the pub. Much of the run-up is a blur of meetings to sort out finances, van hire for removals, Licence transfer applications, inventories of fixtures and fittings, etc. etc. The transfer of Licence involved appearance at Haverfordwest Magistrates Court to obtain a Protection Order to cover the period up to 10 October which was the next Licensing Sessions when my Full Licence could be applied for and granted. I also needed a Gaming Licence for the fruit machine bandit and a *Performing Rights Society* Licence for the Juke Box.

The main part of the 'Ingoing' would be the purchase of all fixtures and fittings connected with the business. Personal property and furniture were excluded but otherwise everything down to the last ash tray and coat hook in the bars, the last fork in the kitchen and the last seat in the garden had to be listed and paid for whether or not it was absolute rubbish and whether or not you actually wanted it. This was done by an independent valuer agreed by both parties, in our case Evans Roach of Haverfordwest with payment by us in advance. Contact with George Dodd was fairly minimal throughout but I have to say that he was fairly normal. Perhaps the thought of leaving had calmed him down or perhaps he was not being troubled by the 'silver plate in his head' that was deemed by many to be his problem.

The actual change-over day 29th September was manic. Dodd's personal property and furniture out, our personal property and furniture in, fixtures and fittings inventory checked by both parties with the valuers and adjusted for anything missing or excluded at the last minute. Glassware inventory to be checked and adjusted. Dry stock – nuts, crisps, sweets, etc. to be scheduled by the valuer. Wet stock to be valued by a representative of James Williams Ltd. Juke box and gaming machine to be checked and emptied by operators (Frank Booth

& Sons, Tenby). Dry stock pre-purchased by us brought in with cash float and change for till in, etc.etc. All this and more and then be ready to open and serve our first customers at 11.00am !

During all this I was horrified to discover that there had been a hold-up in George Dodd's move away and that he had temporarily rented the bungalow directly across the road from the Brook. I tactfully suggested that it would perhaps be best if he didn't become a customer so I had barred someone even before I had opened and ironically it was the man who had barred so many before me. The second horrific discovery was the state of the kitchen. It was on the ground floor, was the only kitchen serving both us and our customers and was so filthy there was no way it could be used. Even with the help of my mother and sister it took days for it to be fit for use with a garden hoe being employed to remove layers of grease and fat from the floor and dustpans literally filled with mouse droppings.

Customers were told that it was closed for 'refurbishment' but with an early microwave behind the bar included in the fixtures and fittings we were at least able to offer warmed up *Bowyer's* pasties and steak & kidney pies which in the event became quite a favourite with our regulars. So before we had taken a penny behind the bar we had laid out on fixtures and fittings, glassware, dry goods stock, wet stock, *Calor* gas stock, proportion of building insurance, share of valuers fee and a brewery bond of £1,500 (returnable when we gave up the tenancy provided all rent and brewery bills were paid) - a total of £4,406.60 plus a bit more on dry stock and equipment – way more than my gross annual salary had been. But we had a loan account, a business account with an overdraft facility and at about thirty seconds past eleven our first customer for whom I pulled my first pint of *Worthington BB* and took from him the princely sum of 29p. I really should remember who it was but I'm afraid I can't. This first pint poured and sold was followed by many more firsts, a good number relating directly to a pint of beer. These included the first spile and tap, first cask tilt, first cask and keg changes, first cask lift, first gas cylinder change, first beer line clean, first complaint about the beer and first compliment on the beer (re-assuringly both on the same day and about pints from the very same cask). It was also re-assuring that none of the complaints came from regular customers who I soon found, given a sample to try in the event of a complaint from a stranger, could be relied upon to declare it excellent. The philosophy was that there is no such thing as a bad pint but some were better than others.

Worthington BB was basically a real ale, (CAMRA fanatics probably wouldn't agree) and was cask conditioned, with a sediment, came in 18 gallon kilderkin casks (kils) and had to be kept on stillage before and during use. The Brook had no cellar, only a bottle, keg and cask store so all keg beers and lagers in use were kept upright under the bar counters. Co2 gas was connected to the keg and the keg connected to the service tap via a cooler. The gas was fed to the bottom of the keg at sufficient pressure to feed the liquid to the service point through the cooler but also to give the beer or lager its bubbles and head. There was no sediment so when a new keg was required it could be rolled, trundled and generally manhandled (often womanhandled) into place and be used immediately. The *BB* was much more demanding.

There was stillage behind the bar – basically a heavy wooden frame just under two feet (60cm) high to accommodate five, possibly six kils horizontally with wooden wedges to keep them steady and in position. There would normally be one in use, one ready for use (two if you were expecting a very heavy session or if the one in use was nearly empty) and the rest 'settling'. Correctly positioned horizontally, the casks would have a large wooden bung at the top (which had been the side when the cask was upright) and a smaller wooden bung at the bottom of the front (which had been the top). To get a kil ready for use it had to be spiled and tapped. The large bung had a pre-cut centre which had to be gently knocked into the cask with a spile tool and mallet, carefully allowing any build up of natural gases to escape very gently and without creating a beer fountain. Once de-gassed and settled, a wooden peg (spile) could be inserted. Then came the exciting bit. The smaller bung at the front was also pre-cut with a larger hole. The tap, always brass, had a fairly long tapered tubular perforated section with a flat end which was held firmly against the bung. The tap then had to be hit just once, with a large rubber mallet at the tap end, hard enough to wedge the tap firmly into the bung but not hard enough to dislodge the cask from its wedges or stir up the sediment in the cask. Then just a couple of more gentle hits to ensure it was firmly bedded.

Done right, it was easy and not a drop would be spilled but if the tap was not held straight or the tap was not hit hard enough or the bung had not been properly pre-cut by *Worthington* or if it was just one of those days, you could very quickly get a beer shampoo, a bar to clean up and some or most of your profit gone. Fortunately all but once or twice I got it totally right or recovered before any real damage was done. Normally tapping a barrel would be something you did only when you were closed but very occasionally on a really busy night, you would need to tap one when the whole world was watching. That's what you call pressure !

When the cask in use came to an end all that had to be done was to connect the beer line to the front of the tap and fit the

Co2 gas supply to the spile hole. We used gas to deliver the beer so that it could go through a cooler. With the heat behind the bar from all the other coolers it would have been impossible to have served the beer from the stillage at a decent temperature. As, unlike kegs, the gas was delivered above the beer (top pressure) there was little reaction between the two and a good pint resulted. If any fanatic really wanted a warm one 'uncontaminated' by gas, we could serve it straight from the tap on the 'ready' cask. However, this wasn't really encouraged as the stooping or bending involved was a bit if a pain.

The 'Good Old Days' – *Worthington BB* **and ashtrays in pubs**

There were two more operations involving *BB* – tilting and lifting. When the cask in use was coming towards its end, it was necessary to very, very gently tilt that cask and support it at the back with a block of wood so that as much as possible of the beer could be drawn off before the sediment was pulled through. Normally the dray men would lift casks onto any empty spaces on the stillage when they made a delivery but quite frequently we needed more stock in a week than the stillage could hold so it would be necessary to roll a cask or two through from the store and lift them up. Eighteen gallons of beer and a metal cask – using the old adage that a pint of water weighs a pound and a quarter you can work out a pretty good estimate of the weight and it's not light. (Sorry, for all you children of the decimal age it works out at about 85kg). I usually did it on my own and my technique must have been fairly good as I only slightly 'did' my back once which was fairly quickly cured by toe touching exercises (Those were the days!)

All day opening in those times was restricted to pubs close to and serving cattle markets and the like, so we had a 'break' of three to four hours in the afternoon when other necessary jobs such as banking takings, visiting the cash & carry, doing the accounts, cutting the grass, etc. etc. etc. could be done and this included another of the firsts, weekly cleaning of the beer lines. It was really very straightforward and involved disconnecting the lines from each keg and cask and connecting each line in turn to a container full of water and cleaning fluid. The beer in the line would be pulled through until clear liquid came through the tap and the lines would be left to soak for a couple of hours before the procedure was reversed. Obviously the beer in the line would be lost and this would be part of the 'Ullage' that the tax man allowed against your profits. Usually though, on the appointed day, I would start the operation immediately after I had called 'Time' on the morning session. On the BB line I would get about a pint and a half of good beer into glasses before reverting to a bucket when the cleaning fluid was abou tto come through. This was shared among any regulars left at the bar and helped with public relations.

14: SETTLING IN

Although we had been thrown in at the deep end, it was probably the best time of year to have been thrown. The Summer rush was over but there would hopefully be some decent local trade up to Christmas and New Year before the traditional lows of January and February. Once the kitchen was finally habitable, Haidee started to offer food. She had decided on a pretty basic menu aimed mainly at lunchtime trade with good value meals and snacks. The target clientele would be drinkers who wanted some food rather than diners who may have a drink and especially in the Summer with a large garden available, families with children looking to feed them without making too big a hole in their holiday spending money. The formula worked well.

James Williams supplied the beer, spirits and soft drinks but we had to connect with or choose suppliers of everything else. Some came to us like Mike Baker the baker with his mobile shop being our source of bread and rolls. A *Bowyers* van called weekly with Wiltshire produced pies, pasties, sausages, etc. James Brothers Butchers called weekly with meat mainly for our own use and our milk was delivered by Arthur and Flo Davies. It seemed that, as with Mr & Mrs Sid Brooks in Dale, you had to be a bit of a character to get up early and deliver milk.

Other things were more specialised. Frank Booth & Sons of Tenby supplied the juke box and gaming machine which were emptied by them regularly and supplied a small but welcome income after rental had been deducted. FC Nicholas Ltd of Haverfordwest provided and filled the cigarette machine and were therefore the obvious choice of supplier for the cigars and rolling tobacco we sold behind the bar. For our heating, Picton Brothers delivered coal and Cartlett Home & Garden Supplies brought *Calor Gas*. Cleaning materials, etc. were covered by Odex Ltd and Stretton Chemical Co. Ltd. West Wales Hotel Supplies provided the £80 worth of glasses we found that we needed in our first week. Local farmer John Llewellin of Bicton Farm provided bags of potatoes and his *Wilja* variety made the best chips ever. For nuts, crisps and virtually everything else it was weekly trips to Gardner's Cash & Carry in Haverfordwest

We started to re-organise things, especially behind the bar, stocking new lines and generally tidying up and this brought me into my first dispute with James Williams. Really delving into how everything worked behind the bar, I realised that the electrics were in a lethal state – for example two coolers and a set of lights all on a three-way adaptor in a single socket which itself was broken and loose. I established that wiring was their responsibility under the tenancy agreement and asked that it be fixed as a matter of urgency. Nothing happened so I contacted them again, once more with no result. We were having to pay the insurance, or at least a proportion, on both building and contents so I contacted them one more time. I said that unless something was done within seven days I would advise the insurance company that the wiring was unsafe when no doubt that would void the policy. As if by magic, an electrician appeared a couple of days later, completely re-wired behind the bar including numerous new sockets and checked everywhere else in the building for safety – Result.

The behind the bar area had serving counters to three rooms – the main public bar, the lounge bar/restaurant and between the two a much smaller room which was rarely used by customers except as a route from the public bar to the ladies. The small room had a large open fire but the two main bars had only *Calor* gas heaters. I was bemoaning this fact chatting to some regulars one lunch time and this led to closer examination, some tapping, the production of a screwdriver and the conclusion that it would be easy. In no time at all the door was off and we could see that the 'wall' consisted of a wooden frame with wallpapered plasterboard on one side and overlapping natural timber planks on the other – typical 1960's. Before I closed for the afternoon it was all gone and all that was required was some carpet patching, a bit of attention to the corner of the bar and a dab of paint here and there and my lovely new 'L' shaped room was ready for the evening session. I gave my three helpers a fiver each (That was about seventeen pints!) and later sold the wood we removed for £10.

Not long afterwards, James Williams' area manager called to collect my cheque for the month's supplies and remarked on what an improvement my changes had made. A few days later however he was back again, this time accompanied by the top man himself, John Davies, who sounded off at great length about how my tenancy agreement specifically denied me authority to remove any wall and how such a breach could lead to immediate termination of my tenancy. I let him run out of steam and then said I had three questions the first of which I would answer myself:- Was it a wall? - No it was a wooden partition. Was the removal an improvement giving much more light, warmth and space? Would it give me the opportunity of selling more of his beer? A few seconds thought was followed by, 'Well, don't do it again'. Not long afterwards in November 1977 our lunchtime customers included two men in a van who had just finished a carpeting contract and had quite a lot left over. Long story short, by the time we opened that evening our 'L' shaped public bar had lovely new matching pub quality carpet throughout courtesy of Mr J Boswell of S C Carpets, his mate and £60 cash in hand.

There was however one regular customer who didn't appreciate the changes. Eddie Edwards was in his late 70s and walked to the pub using two sticks often bearing the grazes and bruises of falls on the way home the night before. If he came in and found someone sitting on 'his' stool he would approach slowly (In fairness that was his only speed), rest heavily on his sticks, glare at them and eventually say, 'You're obviously not from around here boy or you would know that I sit there'. He had been used to propping his sticks up against the partition and leaning on it from 'his' stool so I had some sympathy but not a lot as he had also used the partition both to knock out his pipe and to spit down. No partition, new carpet, problem solved.

Talking of regulars, one lunchtime, I was having a gentle go at two of them about all the benefits they enjoyed as pensioners compared to the working man – not having to get up in the morning, cheap haircuts, bus passes, etc. (I'm not sure if bus passes existed then but you get the idea). Eventually, one of them took the bait and said, 'We fought the war for you young buggers'. His companion agreed loudly, 'That's right we did'. and seemed mystified when I burst out laughing. They had indeed fought the war – Taff Davies as a Corporal in the RAF and Horst Vietze as a Sergeant in the German army! Taff was from another part of Wales, always cheerful and with a lovely sense of humour. I have great memories of him pretending to 'chat up' my straight-laced widowed mother-in-law on one of her visits.

Horst – universally known as 'Veetsie' an approximation of his surname, was an incredible man. When we moved into the Brook, the fixtures and fittings inventory listed 'two caravans, one with mains electricity. What the inventory didn't say was that the one with mains electricity contained a resident German who came with the pub. I was aware that in previous arrangements he had lived rent free in exchange for odd jobs. This was an arrangement we were happy to continue especially as one of the odd jobs was the daily cleaning of the gents toilets which were outside and not particularly salubrious

Veetsie had survived the retreat from Stalingrad when hauling barrage balloons and equipment in incredibly cold conditions they had had to kill and eat their horses to live. He had also survived the fierce fighting at Monte Casino in Italy but his luck had finally run out in France after the D-Day landings when having decided that the game was up he gathered his men together and hid in an orchard. He told them that it was time to surrender but that they would be far better treated if they surrendered to the Americans rather than the British. They stayed concealed for many hours as a number a British formations went by but eventually they heard American accents and he led his men out with hande hoch. Unfortunately their 'Americans' were actually Canadians and after being taken to Canada he was quite quickly shipped back to Scotland. He was moved to POW camps in Kent, Belfast and Carmarthen before finally ending up at Trewarren Camp in St Ishmaels.

He was put to work on the land and after the War he worked at Butterhill and later at Sandyhill Farm, Sandy Haven until he retired. He was originally from Dresden which was in the Russian zone of Germany and having received a letter from a sister he decided to stay in the UK leaving in Germany a wife and two children who he never saw again. When East Germany opened up he received letters from his brother Dieter who had returned to Dresden but Veetsie told me that he had never answered them fearing a 'Russian trap'. The caravan was freezing in Winter, totally unsuitable for someone of his age and I checked to make sure that he was on the council housing waiting list and nagged the council on a frequent basis.

Eventually he was allocated a bungalow in St Ishmaels and also suffered a stroke (I can't remember in which order) and this led to him eventually being reunited with his brother. Ironically, Dieter had also been a POW, had been captured by Americans but had still been sent to Scotland. Horst, when you could get him to talk, had some fascinating stories to tell. His English was very good but sometimes not quite getting the idiom right and I will always remember his description of a dark sky as being 'as black like the ace of spades'.

Another incredible man in those early days was Arthur Bowen. Retired, he would spend most of the day and evening 'on tour' and start pretty early in the morning. Every stop on that tour would involve a drink of some sort and one of those stops was often the Brook. He was the only man I have ever known who could have up to three drinks, all different, going at the same time in different parts of the pub. As he circulated around the bar, various people would offer him a drink and invariably he would ask what they themselves were drinking and would have the same. He would then keep circulating around the drinks he had left in those various places invariably buying drinks in return before leaving. Yet despite all this I never ever saw him the worse for wear. I once said to him, 'Arthur, tell me straight, just how much do you actually drink in a day?' He had a bit of a stutter and his reply was, 'Wwwwell boy, there's ssssome days I has ttttwenty pints and there's other dddddays I has a lot'.

Partition down so we can see Horst Vietze on left, Roy Hill in overalls, Arthur Jenkins wearing glasses and Taff Davies

Among the regulars were Vince Edwards who was the captain of the darts team and welcomed my 'transfer' from the Lobster Pot, was very helpful and became a good friend. Roy Hill from the Valleys, always cheerful and never a complaint. Roy Cheshire another who always had a cheery word. Arthur Jenkins lead tenor whenever we had a sing-song night and who did a memorable version of *Are You Lonesome Tonight*. Harold Thomas from Mullock Farm who brought his piano accordion to the sing-songs and provided the backing. John Hawkins who was Vince's son-in-law and dealt in anything he could acquire cheap and sell on but specialised in taxi driving and selling second hand cars to the American forces at Brawdy on the basis that they were rust free (no extra charge for the rust). Kenny 'Tuts' Thomas who worked at one of the refineries and later spent years in Saudi Arabia. Dai Thomas who liked to tell everyone that he had served in the Welsh Guards (but according to some sources not for very long and most of it AWOL). Dai's brother Adrian known as 'Tarzan' and their father Hugh. Bill Roberts, Head Teacher at the village school whose wife Janice would become a member of our Ladies darts team and later still would marry my brother. Pete John another teacher. Chris Bradshaw who was an engineer officer on the Irish ferry out of Fishguard and was a neighbour of my parents in Brookside. He and his wife Wendy are still in the village and stalwart supporters of the cricket club. Many I have mentioned became fellow darts team members. I could go on and on but I had better stop there for now.

Mention of the sing-songs brings me to about a year after we moved in when, as I could just about get a tune out of a piano, I thought it would be great if we bought an electronic organ that could play all the chords for me. I could make some sort of noise to support the singing and if anyone else was better at it they could have a go too. A visit to *Cranes Music* in Haverfordwest and for £675 we became the proud owners of a *Hammond* organ. Not having that sort of money available we did it on hire purchase (the old name for extended credit). Not long after this I had a telephone call from my bank manager. I thought that he would be lecturing me for taking on more debt but no, he was just really upset that I had gone elsewhere for credit and had not asked him to extend our loan.

Mine Host at the main Bar counter with view through to Lounge Bar counter over my right shoulder

I made mention of regular customers earlier but of course they need staff to serve them. Particularly in the early days, we pretty much kept it in the family other than for Veetsie our inherited handyman. Over the years, some bar staff were with us fairly briefly but two staff members in particular must get a mention. Avril Davies began work behind the bar as soon as she was legally old enough, became very good at it and was with us for some time. Eira Best from the village was for a number of years our very excellent cleaner/general helper who was very thorough, always cheerful and much appreciated. Both became as much friends as employees.

Prior to the electronic organ, our first major purchase had been made earlier when in March 1978 I had finally decided to replace the clapped out, greenish, French, shrunken carpeted *Simca 1500* and had gone to the Auto Trade Centre at Whitland to pay £2095 for a gleaming silver grey P reg. 2.5 litre *Ford Granada.* A much more suitable form of transport for a licensed victualler. Four months later, I added to the transport stable when I went to Greens Motors in Haverfordwest and bought a white *Morris Marina* ex-police dog van for £850 plus VAT. In the best traditions of *Blue Peter* I bought some bright orange *Fablon* sticky-back plastic and designed lettering to cut out and stick *Brook Inn St Ishmaels* on each side of the van giving some nice free advertising on journeys to pick up stock. The van proved to be a great bargain and very useful. Both boys learned to drive in it on Dale airfield long before they were old enough to go on the road and when we left the pub I finally sold it to a farmer up in the Preseli Hills. Years later, I had a report that it had been seen near Maenclochog still advertising the Brook. Why waste all that time peeling letters off – true Pembrokeshire philosophy.

Mine Hostess at the Lounge Bar counter with choice of two lagers

15: PAINT JOB

Things seemed to be moving in the right direction as in December 1977 our weekly takings hit £700 for the first time and between July and September 1978 new highs of £800, £900 and then £1,000 were hit. These are not averages but highs and are the figures shown in our account books and not therefore perhaps totally correct. As far as everything supplied by James Williams was concerned, Inland Revenue worked on the basis of their monthly invoices and calculated tax on what we should have taken or what our books said we had taken, whichever was the higher. Much the same was true of any supplies such as cigarettes and tobacco for which a monthly invoice was received. Food and any stock purchased with cash was very much a different matter and in common with every other licensee I knew, just about half of takings on meals, snacks, crisps and nuts, etc. actually went through the books. As we got braver there was also usually one bottle of spirits on the optics that was 'ours'.

More income was forthcoming when in March 1978 we got rid of all of the rubbish and things we didn't need that we had been forced to buy from George Dodd as part of the ingoing. Frank Dunn, the licensee of the Copper Coins was by now working part-time for Basil Jones & Sons in Haverfordwest and with his help an auction was held in St Ishmaels village hall, mostly of our stuff but with other items also brought in. It was a very successful day as all our items sold and being close by, we had a very nice boost to our morning takings. After VAT, commission and expenses we received a very welcome cheque for £249.67. At the same sale we took the opportunity to rid ourselves of the now unwanted Simca 1500. I have no memory of how much it made but I doubt it was a great deal. I must have caught the auction bug as a few months later I went to another Basil Jones sale and bought two antique hay grabs and a horse harrow to decorate the pub garden for a total of £5.40 which I thought was a great bargain until I had to move them every time I cut the grass. We also invested in a quantity of chairs, stools and benches for the bars and a filing cabinet for my little office upstairs all from A.George Edwards who operated from a warehouse on Milford Docks. George specialised in MoD surplus furniture, etc. much of which was ex-married quarters and was very good quality. I bought an oak desk for my parents which my sister Jennifer has to this day. George was the uncle of Welsh rugby legend Gareth Edwards who I met on one of his fairly frequent visits.

Another source of small but steady income were the juke box and gaming machine (always called the bandit although it didn't have an arm, only buttons). The machines were supplied by Frank Booth & Sons of Tenby and were emptied by them fortnightly. A fairly typical yield for the two weeks would be bandit £75 and juke box £15 which, after Frank Booth, James Williams and the VAT man had taken their slices, would leave around £35 for us before Income Tax. This was massively boosted by one man – Bill Collett Snr. father of Bill Collett who ran the Sunnyside Garage & Filling Station in the village. Known as 'old Bill' to distinguish him from his son, he was a fairly regular customer particularly at lunchtimes when sometimes but not always, he would play the bandit like a real addict, feeding coins in as fast as he could, sometimes even missing wins in the process. I used to keep an unusually large 'float' of change just for him as he would fairly often change two or even three £5 notes in a session.

Old Bill had once lived in the smallholding next to Leatherslade Farm in Buckinghamshire, the lair of the Great Train Robbers in 1963 and was resident there at the time of the robbery. He never seemed to be short of cash and rumours often circulated that he had received a backhander for turning a blind eye at the time. All gaming machines were set to pay out a certain percentage of what was fed in and old Bill sometimes hit the jackpot but never as frequently as he should. Number two son Douglas soon worked this out and when he got off the bus from Milford Grammar, his first question would be, 'Has old Bill been in – did anybody win?' Given the right answer, i.e. Bill had put loads in without anyone winning a jackpot, he would rush upstairs, collect his own 'float' and play (the bar was of course closed at this time) until the jackpot he knew was due duly dropped. This became a very useful supplement to his pocket money.

The juke box was played less frequently and was switched off altogether during league darts matches. Frank Booth & Sons supplied two new records only at a time – I can't remember whether it was fortnightly or monthly – taking off those that had been played least. Sometimes when a good hit had not been supplied we would buy it ourselves and put it in the machine. The box was a *Wurlitzer* with really good sound quality and would probably be worth a lot of money now. The Number One when we moved in was *Yes Sir I Can Boogie* by Baccara which was played a lot and which I still like. Other frequent plays over the years we were at the Brook included of course Abba with *Take A Chance On Me, Name Of The Game, Super Trouper* and *The Winner Takes It All,* etc. the fabulous Debbie Harry & Blondie with *The Tide Is High*, *Atomic*, and *Heart Of Glass* and (we were in Wales) Shakin' Stevens with *Green Door* and *This 'Ole House.*

There were always a number of Elvis Presley discs left in the juke box permanently and of course (we were in Wales) some by Tom Jones, Shirley Bassey and Bonnie Tyler. Among the others I remember with pleasure or which are seared upon my memory are: *Matchstalk Men And Matchstalk Cats And Dogs* by Brian & Michael, *Rivers Of Babylon* by Boney M, *Imagine* by John Lennon, *A Little Peace* by Nicole, *Come On Eileen* by Dexy's Midnight Runners, *Video Killed The Radio Star* by Buggles, *Pass The Dutchie* by Musical Youth, *Bright Eyes* by Art Garfunkle, *Making Your Mind Up* by Bucks Fizz, *Coward Of The County* by Kenny Rogers and *Love Is In The Air* by John Paul Young. I suppose there could have been much worse periods in time to have a juke box as part of your life.

So, we were well settled in, making improvements and changes, had some very good part-time staff and helpers including my Dad who had appointed himself head cleaner of brasses and windows provided that he could do it while we were open in the morning so that he could combine the work with chatting to all and sundry. The big downside was the condition of the outside of the premises. When we moved in, the 'white' wall covering was peeling and discoloured, paintwork generally was in a terrible condition, the black wooden shutters were rotten and disintegrating and there was no proper pub sign. In desperation, I had hand painted a sign on an old door and propped it against the entrance to the public bar. All this was the responsibility of James Williams and despite monthly requests nothing had been done and every month it got worse.

At last, I conceded defeat and asked if I could do it myself. Of course I could! Having seen how badly my white finish had weathered and how quickly other buildings locally deteriorated and discoloured when painted white, I decided that I should paint it any colour except white. I wanted something fairly bright and attractive but which would weather well, last long and not show marks. After literally minutes of research I chose a *Dulux Weathershield* shade that I can best describe as golden brown with the window frames etc. brilliant white. I set to work and just ripping the rotten black shutters down made the place look better. I did most of the work myself but with a bit of help from coastguard volunteers used to climbing cliffs on the gable ends and chimneys. Two and in some places, three coats later and I was very happy with the result.

In very tatty white and black. View from garden with new Ford Grenada at side and rear view with Brook van.

Not so happy was the James Williams area manager on his next visit. 'What have you done?' he asked, 'All James Williams houses are white and black'. I replied that this one wasn't and suggested that if they had paid for it as I had repeatedly asked, they could have chosen the colour and that if they really wanted it white they were welcome to come and repaint it. It stayed golden brown. There were a few moans in the village because the Brook had 'always been white'. Actually it had mostly been grey or off-white at best and the majority approved although many years later it became white again.

'Tish Carnival procession paused outside the Brook before our paint job

After our first year, we had taken a very short holiday leaving a couple we knew well in charge. As far as we were concerned, they had done a good job. Takings were at or just above what we would have expected, everything was clean and tidy, all the beer was in good condition and as far as we knew everything had gone smoothly. Then some of the regulars started moaning. Silly little things like, 'they were five minutes late opening', 'they didn't light the fire at the right time', 'they forgot to close the curtains', 'they did this', 'they didn't do that' and on and on. We felt that this was a manifestation of the relationship that pub regulars often have with 'their' landlord or landlady, that they have some sort of ownership in them and feel deprived if they are left with a stand-in. When you leave the pub for good, that's fine because they have new permanent replacements but take a

The new golden brown paint job (The strange pose was due to a game of cricket with the boys)

That first break away had been for just four nights in October 1978 when we took the boys to the Webbington Country Club at Loxton near Weston-Super-Mare. I had discovered the Webbington on a boys night out from my CID course in Bristol when female impersonators, exotic dancers and strippers formed the entertainment. I had however established that some of their performers were more family friendly and perhaps more suitable for teenaged boys. We had a great time with visits to Cheddar Gorge and Wookey Hole but the real highlight was the

One Night Only performance by *Slade* supported by *Paper Lace* who belted out *Billy Don't Be A Hero*. Noddy Holder, Dave Hill and the rest of *Slade* were superb. We all loved it and the sound was such that I actually felt my diaphragm vibrate.

After that we decided that in future we should take separate holidays. I was the first beneficiary when in 1979 I spent 7 nights in Tenerife with my brother Nigel. This was my first trip abroad since at age 15, I had been on a school trip to Switzerland. It was also the start of a love affair with Puerto de La Cruz that lasted until 2012 when I made my 16th visit. The following year I flew out to join my brother and his mate in Malta and Haidee took the boys to Benidorm. In 1980 the boys did very well going to Majorca with Haidee and her mother and to Puerto de La Cruz, Tenerife with me extended from 7 to 10 days for the first time. It was perhaps a sign of things to come that there were no more foreign holidays from the Brook after this.

When our first tax return was about to become due we made what turned out to be the excellent decision to employ an accountant and chose Ashmole & Company of Victoria Place, Haverfordwest where we were looked after by Cliff Reynolds. He proved to be a great help on our first visit with such questions as, 'Do you buy a daily paper. Do your customers read it? - Deductible', 'Do you pick flowers from your garden and put them in the bars? - Deductible'. One year we had a letter from the tax man saying that they had evidence of undeclared income and asking us to declare it. We were totally mystified but fairly worried that it may have something to do with the food. Inland Revenue steadfastly refused to say what the income was or who their source was. We contacted Cliff and by some mysterious contact he managed to find out that they were talking about Littlewoods Pools. It then finally dawned on us that we had been collecting customers football pools coupons as 'part of the service' and taking them in weekly to an area collector in Milford usually at the same time as going to the bank. For this we were paid a minuscule commission. Cliff convinced the Revenue that this income was almost totally offset by the cost of petrol and depreciation on the van. Everyone was happy and we gave a sigh of relief.

>
> 25th October to 28th October
>
> **PAPER LACE**
> Great Recording Group
> Mem. Guests T/M
> Wed 50p 75p £1.00
> Fri/Sat 75p £1.00 £1.00
>
> One night only:
> Wednesday 25th Oct.
> **SLADE**
> Admission £2.00
>
> 29th October to 4th November

Top of the bill at the Webbington

May 1979 saw the election of Councillors to serve on Preseli District Council and I decided to stand. The sitting member was Cllr. Herbert John 'Bertie' Edwards of Haven High, St Anne's Head. Bertie was apparently no great lover of incomers and had been considerably less than helpful when my sister had moved to Pembrokeshire and was seeking council accommodation having been made homeless with six children by her divorce. I knew that I had almost certainly no chance of winning but I think he had been returned unopposed at the previous election and I thought that at least I would make him work for it this time.

I was proposed by my brother Nigel, seconded by Bill Roberts and my other signatories included pub customers Vince Edwards, Chris Bradshaw and Ray Lewis, my old Lobster Pot darts skipper Billy Price from St Brides, Audrey Oldham and Bob Medway from Dale and Anne Rees. Bertie's signatories included Graham Sutton which surprised me and Ray Procter from St Ishmaels which didn't. I lost but for the price of a few leaflets (buying beer would have been illegal!) I had a lot of fun, gave Bertie a fright and made the bugger work for his seat.

16: *MISTER TOWN CLERK*

Since moving to the Brook, I had carried on as Clerk to Marloes Community Council as the duties were hardly arduous, just a monthly evening meeting and dealing with correspondence. The pub was now running very smoothly and to be honest Winter weekday lunchtimes with virtually the same customers every day were becoming just a little bit boring. I was quite interested therefore when in November 1979 I saw an advertisement for the post of part-time Clerk & Financial Officer to Pembroke Town Council. They were offering £2,822 rising to £3,292 for a 20 hour week, mostly mornings with two evening meetings a month. I thought that this would fit very well with the pub, especially as the meeting nights weren't darts nights, and banged in an application.

I was quite surprised when I was one of a short-list of four to be interviewed by the full council on 27 November and even more surprised when I was offered the job. The only doubts were raised by Cllr Phyllis Peachey who was herself a pub landlady and when she asked me how I could run a pub and do a part-time job, she seemed satisfied with my reply that I had an excellent wife and great staff who had been trained to do things our way. The job was currently being done by two people – Miss Audrey Humphreys who was Town Clerk and Desmond Lowless who was Financial Officer and I would work in tandem with them for the first month to learn the ropes.

This was a role reversal as in his previous job Col. R. Desmond Lowless M.B.E. had been Town Clerk to the former Pembroke Borough Council and Miss Humphreys had been his Deputy. Desmond Lowless was quite a character and had got his M.B.Ei n 1945 after serving with the Royal Artillery in Italy. He was very prominent locally – founder President of Pembroke Rotary Club,etc. etc. and would be a very hard act to follow. Miss Humphreys was much quieter but very pleasant and welcoming and I often wondered if they had ever been anything other than just work colleagues. I was quite amused when at the first council meeting I attended, Mr Lowless having done his bit by presenting the financial report, stood up and spent the rest of the meeting wandering around the council chamber loudly puffing and tutting at anything said he considered to be stupid (a lot apparently). I'm not sure whether he always did this or whether it was because he was retiring.

In the Council Chamber – I would normally have been seated at the table in front of the Mayor

Now if you had been paying attention at the start of Chapter 12, you will be aware that under the Local Government Act 1972, Pembroke Town Council would have been a Community Council which had resolved to call itself a Town Council and style its Chairman as Town Mayor but unlike some Town Councils it was the direct successor of the former Pembroke Borough Council which Miss Humphreys and Col. Lowless had served. However unlike some Town Councils, it didn't actually do much. It didn't for example provide and operate open spaces, play areas or playing fields, it didn't operate and administer a cemetery, it didn't choose to supply and maintain litter bins, public seats bus shelters or street furniture, it didn't operate a swimming pool or leisure centre, it didn't operate a community complex with meeting rooms, auditorium and licensed bar, etc. etc. all of which councils at this level could do, which is why my post was part-time.

The Town Council had a small first floor office at 8A Castle Terrace on the approach to Pembroke Castle, operated the Town Hall in Main Street and a public hall, the Pater Hall, in Pembroke Dock. Although called Pembroke Town Council, it covered what were in effect, the two towns of Pembroke and Pembroke Dock. All staff were part-time with two receptionists/typists who also did wages and accounts, a cleaner and myself covering the office and the Town Hall together with a caretaker and cleaner at the Pater Hall. One of the two ladies in the office, Carmel Wiseman, taught me far more about how things operated than the two I was replacing whose contributions were more or less on the lines of 'You'll soon pick it up.' Equal numbers of Councillors were elected from each of the Pembroke and Pembroke Dock (Pater) Wards and it had become a tradition that the office of Mayor should alternate annually between Pembroke and Pembroke Dock members.

Council's main tasks therefore were operating its own buildings, statutory comment on planning applications, responding to consultations and correspondence and seeking to ensure that the town got the best possible service from the District Council, the County Council and other public bodies. Our meetings alternated between the Town Hall in Pembroke and the District Council Offices in Pembroke Dock and I soon discovered that if Pembroke had a pothole that needed mending, then Pembroke Dock would have to have one too and if Pembroke Dock had a street light unlit then no doubt there would be one not working in Pembroke as well. What the Council did do however and did very well as it had been doing it for well over half a millennium, was Civic Ceremonial. My first Mayor, Cllr. Brian Phillips, was Pembroke's six hundredth!

The Council's Annual Meeting, often known as 'Mayor Making' was always held in May and always at 12.00 noon in the Courtroom in the Town Hall rather than the Council Chamber so that all guests could be accommodated and it was a long guest list with virtually every organisation and club in the town represented and always a guest of honour. The outgoing Mayor in full robes and chain, outgoing Deputy Mayor, Mayor-elect, and me as Town Clerk would occupy 'The Bench' with the rest of Council members in the front row below them. After some preliminaries with the outgoing Mayor in the Chair, the new Mayor would be duly elected and would withdraw with the outgoing Mayor and Town Clerk to the Mayor's Parlour where the robes and jabot would be removed from one and placed on the other. I usually kept a spare jabot so that the new mayor would have something clean and unsweaty round their neck and gave a hand with putting on the robes the fastenings of which would be unfamiliar to them..

I would retain the chain and the outgoing Mayor would return to the Bench. After a suitably dramatic pause, I would call for all present to stand for the new Mayor. He (or she) preceded by two uniformed Mace Bearers would enter and take the Chair to have the chain placed about their shoulders by the outgoing Mayor to the accompaniment of polite applause. My job then was to ensure that the chain was in the right place, invariably having to adjust it, and to tie the ribbons on the robes that held it there. The Mayor would now make a speech of acceptance, call for the election of the Deputy Mayor, appoint his Mayoress (or her Consort) and appoint the Mayor's Chaplain before adjourning all other business to the next meeting of Council.

That was just the start! Virtually all present would then make their way to the next event, the Mayoral Civic Luncheon. During my time it was mostly held at the Cleddau Bridge Hotel but there was one rather more down market occasion when the incoming Mayor insisted that it should be held in the Pater Hall, Pembroke Dock. Outside caterers were used on this occasion and so typical of local caterers in those days they provided a prawn cocktail starter and an ice cream gateau desert. I had to earn my lunch by acting as Toastmaster. The guest of honour at the end of his speech (and it was always a male then) would propose the toast 'Pembroke Town Council' and the Mayor would respond. Then a senior Councillor, usually a previous Mayor, would propose the toast 'Our Guests' and a pre-selected guest would respond. Once the speeches were over, plates cleared and glasses drained it was time for a quick dash home, me change into dinner jacket and Haidee into a second posh frock and off to the Mayoral Ball, again usually held, in my time, at the Cleddau Bridge Hotel although I remember when Charlie Thomas became Mayor in 1981 his was at the Palladium Ballroom. (That was Pennar Park not New York 53rd St).

Even more guests would be invited to the Mayor's Ball as it was informally known and it was always a fun event. Those who had been involved in the two previous events of the day could finally relax and those who hadn't could enjoy the fact that everything, apart from their drinks, was free. One memory stands out above all others of the Mayor's Ball. We had a civic link with HMS Pembroke in Chatham (more of which later) and the Commanding Officer and others were invited to the Ball. The first of these I knew was Captain Ken Wilcockson who enjoyed the event so much that even after he had been promoted and moved on, asked if he and his wife could still come. Of course we said yes, which led to my enduring memory. If you had ever seen a Rear Admiral in full dress uniform including sword doing a *'Chicken Dance'* to *The Birdie Song* by The Tweets, you would have never forgotten it either. Ken was promoted in 1981 and in 1982 at the time of the Falklands conflict he was in charge of the MoD department that looked after the welfare of victims and their families. Obviously a stressful job that really needed relaxation when possible and perhaps contributed to his early death. Ken(neth) Dilworth East Wilcockson C.B.E. (1927-1986), a truly lovely man, R.I.P.

But, after the fun, the ceremonial still wasn't over. On the first Sunday after Mayor making a Civic Service would be held in the church or chapel where the new Mayor usually worshipped (or selected if he/she wasn't a usual God botherer) and where the Mayor's Chaplain appointed by him or her presided. So it was full robes and best suits and frocks again but this time followed by a much more informal withdrawal to a nearby pub by some of those present. Each year, a sum would be set aside in Council's financial estimates as the 'Mayor's Allowance' and all the costs of the Lunch, Ball and Civic Service would be taken from this. What was left was intended to help the Mayor with costs for the rest of the year and when everything was paid, as Financial Officer, I would write them a cheque for the balance. This would always be very small and on more than one occasion the Mayor had to write me a cheque to cover overspend. This left them with the rest of a year in which they would receive two or three invitations a week from local groups and organisations to events where they would almost certainly be expected to put their hand in their pocket for raffle tickets, a purchase from a stall or a donation. Then there was the need to buy suitable clothes for such events. Being elected Mayor cost a lot of money in Pembroke in those days.

Going back to the Civic Lunches. I remember four of the five main guests who I had the pleasure of introducing as toastmaster (apologies to the non-memorable performer). One was Captain Patrick 'Paddy' Sheehan who had followed Ken Wilcockson as Commanding Officer at HMS Pembroke (more of whom later). Another, at the downmarket Pater Hall, was Lord Parry of Neyland, then Chairman of the Wales Tourist Board who I had previously known as Gordon Parry a former teacher from Neyland who had stood three times as Labour Party candidate for the Pembrokeshire parliamentary constituency and who had come second each time. His reward for keeping on trying was a Life Peerage from Labour leader James Callaghan. My sister knew his daughter The Hon. Cathy Parry Sherry before she was honourable (if you know what I mean).

The third was Clive Thomas from the Rhondda Valley, Group Executive of Office Cleaning Services Ltd. I wasn't particularly impressed until the Mayor-elect told me that the person she was inviting was actually THE Clive Thomas – probably the most controversial international football referee ever. He had possibly reached the summit of his fame or infamy four years earlier at the 1978 World Cup in a game between Brazil and Sweden.

The score was 1-1 when Brazil took a corner kick which was nodded in by Zico to give Brazil victory. But no, with just six seconds of added time on the clock, Thomas had blown the final whistle while the ball was still mid-air – No goal. He was very much a *Marmite* referee, love him or hate him but he was a pretty good speaker.

The fourth speaker I remember is John H Barrett who in 1947 had become the first Warden of the Dale Fort Field Study Centre and was instrumental in establishing the Skokholm Island Bird Observatory. Serving in RAF Bomber Command he was shot down early in WW2 and spent the rest of the war in various POW camps including Stalag Luft III where he was part of the support team for the famous 'Wooden Horse' escape. 'JB' as he was known, left the RAF with the rank of Wing Commander soon after the war to pursue the interest in natural history that he had developed as a prisoner. He played a considerable part in the establishment of the Pembrokeshire Coast National Park and served on its committee for 25 years writing the HMSO official guide to the Park. He was the author of many books and papers including *The Pembrokeshire Coast Path* and *A Plain Man's Guide To The Path Round The Dale Peninsular* which we found very useful and informative when we made our first circumnavigation soon after moving there. JB had stayed on in Dale after his retirement, was an active member of Dale Sailing Club and served on the Parish Council. I was quite pleased that while chatting after the lunch he acknowledged me as a former fellow Dale resident and praised my contribution to the village. That was my last Civic Lunch in Pemboke and a good one to finish on.

17: *MEANWHILE, BACK AT THE BROOK*

When we first moved into the Brook, we were often asked whether we had seen Gladys yet. Gladys was the almost legendary former landlady of the pub who was said to haunt the place. Gladys had lived all her life at the Brook. Her father Thomas Hughes had been landlord from 1910 until his death in 1948 when Gladys had taken over. In 1952 she had married John Dillon (whose death and dog I described in Chapter 7) but she was only ever referred to as Gladys Hughes. She stayed as licensee of the Brook until the late 1960s and always kept a pig in the garden which was fed on scraps and beer slops from the pub and was presumably therefore always happy. Every year a day was set aside for the slaughter of the pig, which was always called Dennis, and crowds would gather to help. Obviously a few drinks were in order before the job was started which on more than one occasion led to a stay of execution for Dennis until the following day or perhaps longer. Even in my time if you asked a more elderly customer whether he wanted the drop of beer left in his glass at the end of a session, the reply would sometimes be, 'No - give it to Dennis.'

Both my parents, when they lived in Bedfordshire, had according to them, each seen ghosts on separate occasions. I had not and was, to say the least, very sceptical but one night something happened that made me wonder. I got up to go to the toilet and as usual, in order not to disturb anyone didn't turn on any lights – it wasn't pitch dark and it was a very short route to the bathroom. As I left the bedroom, I saw what I can only describe as a female shape walking along ahead of me. This couldn't be possible as the female shape was walking straight and level in mid-air above the stairs. The shape then turned left and disappeared. I made it to the bathroom and looked very carefully when I came out but there was nothing other than the empty stairs to see. It did however feel very real especially when the following morning I remembered that the stairs had been moved by a previous tenant and where the shape was walking would have been flat floor in Gladys's time. Some years later, when we were in our last few weeks at the pub, my son Douglas was in the bar holding a pint glass with two hands when suddenly it was knocked out of his grasp – by nobody. Vince Edwards witnessed this and his immediate reaction was 'Bloody Hell', followed by 'Looks like Gladys doesn't want you to go.'

Gladys wasn't a regular I'm pleased to say but perhaps now it's time to remember a few more that were. Some we had from the start and kept throughout and others we gained over the years often when they moved into the village. Among the latter were Tony and Freda Gordon who had moved into Brookside and were neighbours of my parents. Tony had worked abroad a lot and used to surprise everybody by saying that the tropical paradise of The Seychelles was a 'horrible place to live'. He was mostly a lunchtime customer who always sat at the bar, happy to chat to anyone as he chain-smoked himself through a couple of pints. Every few days he would 'take out' a 2 litre plastic container of 'English Sherry' which I got for him from the cash & carry (He was my only customer for this particular line!). Sometimes on a Sunday he would leave with a small bottle of *Britvic Orange* saying that Freda was 'cooking duck a-l'orange'.

Freda sometimes came in with Tony and occasionally on her own when her particular 'take out' would often be a packet of *Smith's Scampi Fries* as they would 'do for old Tony's lunch'. I can't believe that *Smiths* still actually sell these things. Freda's other claim to fame was her ability to give her car absolutely maximum revs and slip the clutch making at least as much noise as a car on a F1 starting grid every single time she got in the car and drove off. The chain smoking eventually cost Tony a lung but that didn't slow him down and he carried on lighting up cigarettes and seeing off the 'English Sherry'.until the Big C got the other lung and him.

At one time Tony was taking flying lessons and to help with the costs he would invite friends to pay for a ride in the back seat of the plane. My first time in a light aircraft was so different to the holiday jets I was used to, hardly seeming to move and I enjoyed a lovely time as we over-flew St Ishmaels then Pembroke Castle and sections of coastline. A later flight wasn't so much fun when an engine fault on the landing approach to Withybush airfield saw the instructor take over and make an emergency landing in a field.

Another good customer and frequent 'take-away' purchaser was Sonia Aldred who had moved to the village from Marloes. She was always good company and ready to chat but often left with a quarter bottle of vodka to 'see her through'.Unfortunately the vodka probably also saw her off and she died in 1985 aged just 39. A very good teller of stories and jokes was Jack Whip but he could never go for more than a week without telling you that he was 'from Burnley' and invariably dispelling any doubt by making sure we knew that that was 'Buurnlegh, Lancs.' Also from England was Bill Dunlop who joined one of our darts teams and was always good company despite having the misfortune to be a supporter of Brentford FC. An early evening regular was Affie John from Marloes who always seemed torn between the need to get to his next port of call and the worry that he may have missed a bit of local gossip by leaving too soon. A good source of that gossip and another early evening caller was John Bowen who also had a very dry sense of humour. I could go on and probably will later.

The opposite to regulars were the holidaymakers who formed a very important part of our trade. Most were very pleasant and no trouble at all but some could be a bit of a pain in the backside. The great advantage though was that you knew that however good or bad they were, they would only be with you for one of two weeks at the most. Lunchtimes were usually the busiest as far as food was concerned and even with three or four in the kitchen and serving (often out to the garden) there could sometimes be a short wait for food. The great majority understood and were quite happy but there were always some who had to have a moan and to my delight there was always at least one every season who would come to the bar and demand, 'How long will my sausages be?' Whereupon I could smile sweetly, hold up both my index fingers and say, 'About that long – they're Jumbos'.

I think it was in our third summer that I put up a list of 'Additional Charges' behind the bar for all to see. I can't remember exactly what was on it but it read something like my version on the next page. People looked at the sign and laughed thinking it was a great joke but in some really deserving cases we applied at least that much and everyone asking for a glass with a handle was always asked 'right or left handed?' It was amazing how many told us in all seriousness. I am reminded that whenever someone ordered a *Manns Brown*, I would usually respond by asking, 'A man's brown what?'

ADDITIONAL CHARGES

Pointing at casks on stillage and asking for a pint of 'that stuff'	10p
Keeping bar staff waiting in the middle of a round (per 20 sec.)	2p
Going to see what Granny wants	10p
Waiting until staff have picked up a glass before asking for 'one with a handle'	5p
Not saying please or thank you	5p
Being from Scotland	2p
Telling us you are from Scotland	5p

If it was holidaymakers that helped takings during the Summer it was darts that were essential in the Winter. I inherited one team which I joined but in following seasons we had two mens teams and a ladies team. The new 'B' Team was formed around Bob Dennison and his sons Dickie and Dai from Milford and skippered by Ernie – I don't think I ever knew his surname. As soon as he was old enough (nearly) to legally go into pubs my son Douglas joined and together with his brother Bill was very well 'looked after' by the rest of the team and never drank (too much).

Brook 'B' Darts team – Doug & Bill on left, Captain Ernie in red jacket, Bill Dunlop next to Bill and Bob Dennison and two sons in back row

Both mens teams played in the Coastal League which had been formed after a breakaway from the Haverfordwest League and meant less travelling and avoiding some less than salubrious venues. With three teams based at the St Ishmaels Sports & Social Club there were plenty of local derbys and I also got to play against my old team at the Lobster Pot. The ladies team was a new venture for the Brook and members included my wife Haidee and my mother Betty and others who come to mind are Sonia Aldred, Janice Roberts, Ida Griffiths from Marloes and her daughter Julie.

Mention of non-salubrious venues reminds me of one night when I was playing for the Lobster Pot in a particularly grotty pub in Haverfordwest and none of us were particularly looking forward to it. As we went in, one of our number noticed the electricity fuse board just inside the front door and deftly threw the off switch plunging the pub into darkness. He went straight to the bar, told the landlord that he was an electrician (he wasn't) and that he would see what he could do. Minutes later, the lights miraculously came back on. It cheered us up greatly, our teammate had at least one free pint from behind the bar and we won.

At the old Welcome Traveller at Tiers Cross, before a game could start, an interior door had to be lifted off its hinges so that the oche could be the right distance from the board and there was no way that all the members of both teams could be in the room at the same time. One night there with the Brook team our after-match sandwiches had been left on a tray covered with a none too white tea cloth. The home team disappeared into the other bar and I think it was Kenny Thomas who theatrically removed the tea cloth to reveal the delicacies beneath but also to release a large swarm of flies that had obviously gained access to our supper through a hole in the cloth. Suddenly no-one was very hungry. Probably the strangest snack offering ever was at the Vine in Johnson when every sandwich had the same filling – cold, un-cooked black pudding!

Darts nationally was very popular around this time and both the Sports & Social Club and the Copper Coins staged exhibition matches with the very top British players taking on selected players from the Coastal League. Our visitors included players like Alan Glazier and the first four BDO World Champions Leighton Rees, John Lowe, Eric Bristow and Jocky Wilson. I played all of these except Jocky Wilson and lost but I did get the man of the match award for coming closest to beating Alan Glazier. Leighton Rees was very popular being the first ever World Champion and of course being Welsh but was a very pleasant down to earth man. John Lowe wasn't known as 'Gentleman John' for nothing because he was just that, a quietly spoken man who was very friendly with no airs and graces whatsoever despite never losing.

I played 'Crafty Cockney' Eric Bristow twice and he was quite a character. In one match at the Copper Coins he hit a good score of 140 or 180 early in the opening game and our 'caller' gave the score in his normal way. Eric turned to him and said, 'Come on mate if I get a good score, let them know. Give it a bit of wellie'. Eric's very next throw was not quite so good and our caller in a very loud voice yelled out, 'TWENTYSIX'. Eric's glare soon turned into a smile and he joined in the laughter of those of us closest to the stage. Again, one of the boys and a nice bloke. Not in that category was Jocky Wilson, a pig of a man. I didn't play him but saw him 'perform' at the Sports Club. Obviously the worse for drink, he lost a game, became increasingly stroppy and eventually stormed off the stage early refusing to play against a woman. If he got any of his fee that night he shouldn't have – just a horrible slob of a man.

I was just an average player really but I once went a whole season undefeated playing in the league for the Brook. There was some skill involved obviously but it was mostly about confidence. If you just 'know' that you are going to hit that winning double and just as importantly, if your opponent knows that you have been enjoying a good run of wins, you are almost there before you throw a dart. As a result of all this I was selected to play for the Coastal League in the Pembrokeshire Super League and with my very first throw at this level hit a maximum 180 on stage at Kiln Park, Tenby. That was probably the peak of my darts career but I was picked once as Sub for Pembrokeshire 'B' entitling me to a Pembrokeshire badge to add to my Coastal badge.

Badges were very much the thing in those days and we had embroidered badges made for our Brook teams.

County & League Badges

At the end of that 'magic' season I decided that I really didn't have the time, the inclination (or the skill) to carry on in the Super League and just played for the Brook and for myself in the once a season Landlords' Cup.

Apart from badges, the real essentials were the 'new' tungsten darts which were, to say the least, not cheap. I remember feeling quite guilty about spending so much when I bought my set in Haverfordwest but they did improve my game and I still have them despite not using them for many years. I did make a little bit against the cost by stocking packs of plastic dart flights and selling them over the bar at a small profit (I still have about twenty packs left if anyone is interested). The other thing about the game of darts was its miraculous effect on people's mental arithmetic. Present some players with a simple column of figures to add up and they would shy away in horror but ask them to add up in their head double top, treble eighteen and five then subtract that total from 501 – no problem – instant.

Collectors Item ?

Moving from the darts season to the potato season, Pembrokeshire Earlies were a very big thing in those days with many more fields planted than nowadays. This attracted buyers and probably the most important of those was attracted to the Brook. Guy Morton was connected to the family that produced *Morton's Peas* and other canned vegetables. He came from Lincolnshire but for several weeks in the potato picking season he would base himself in a rented property in St Ishmaels. He would fly to it in his own helicopter which he would then use to go from farm to farm buying up new potatoes. His luggage and other necessary equipment would follow on one of the several lorries that were part of his operation. Among the vital equipment carried down from his home would be his electronic organ which he liked to play for relaxation.

We had upgraded our second hand *Hammond* organ, which had proved to be a success, to a new *Yamaha* which did quite a bit more and son Douglas had taken an interest becoming quite proficient at playing it when the pub was closed. On one of his visits for a quiet pint Guy learned about this and straight away invited Doug to 'come and have a go on mine' whenever he liked. The invitation was accepted and really enjoyed because to put it into the automotive terms of those days, if the *Hammond* had been a *Mini-van*, our *Yamaha* would have been a *Ford Escort* and Guy's organ would have been an *Aston Martin* with every available optional extra.

Guy's home was obviously quite something as one day, without any pretentiousness or false modesty he casually remarked that the village cricket team played in his back garden. Guy was a very nice man, generous without being flashy and very much down to earth. For example his helicopter was never for bragging or posing, just a tool to help him do the job. Both of Guy's sons followed him into the potato trade and in the 1990s they were trading as Guy Morton & Sons out of March in Cambridgeshire. Now Nick Morton is a consultant with NM Potato Procurement Specialists in Peterborough and the elder son Steve is Wholesale Director of Linwood Crops in March, a successor of Morton Beeson & Manchett where Steve developed the brand *Guy's Fries* which you may well be offered with your burger.

Time for an update on the vehicle front. I had been very happy with the *Ford Granada* but in July 1980, it needed some work doing and I allowed John Hawkins to talk me into buying a replacement from him rather than having it repaired. It was a *Vauxhall Victor 1800 Estate* TML 662S priced at £2950 against which John gave me £1700 for the *Ford*. It was probably the worst deal I ever made. In fairness to John, the *Vauxhall* was immaculate, finished in an unusual dark brown and in perfect mechanical order. It would have been an excellent replacement for the Brook van but for the *Granada* – no way. The estate gearing meant that it would chug along all day but after the *Granada* it was totally dead and had no performance whatsoever. Less than three months later on 15 October 1980, we went to W P Lewis & Son at Pembroke Dock and bought an *Opel Ascona 2.0S* in Jade Green, registration XBX 803T priced at £3850. I lost over a thousand pounds on part exchanging the *Victor* but it was worth it. The *Ascona* was one of the best cars I ever owned with great performance and excellent road holding. I kept it for almost seven years.

Another purchase from John Hawkins was a new-fangled digital watch. It had probably fallen off the back of a lorry state-side and cost £40 – quite a lot of money but he only had three and was keeping one of those for himself because they were so good. It was shiny chrome with a black face and a red digital display. It was very posy indeed, kept perfect time and was fine at night or indoors but as soon as you got outside in any kind of brightness, never mind full sun, it was impossible to read and virtually useless. I got fed up after a while and just threw it into a drawer. Only a couple of years ago, I re-discovered the watch and checked it out on the internet. I found that it was worthless but that it was a sought-after design icon and that had I bothered to take the battery out before discarding it so that it didn't corrode, it would have been worth anything between £800 and £1,000!

Earlier that year, in March I decided to give up my very part-time job as Clerk to Marloes Community Council and this was in no way connected to what was probably the most embarrassing mistake in any of my Local Government careers. Honestly and truthfully, I only discovered it after I had resigned and just before my replacement took over. Visitors, tradesmen and delivery drivers were often having trouble finding Gaylane Terrace because it wasn't signed despite it being probably the largest housing development in the village. Preseli District Council was responsible for street name plates but refused to help on the legitimate grounds that the terrace was just a development on part of Gay Lane which was the main road up to and through the village I advised Marloes Council that it had the powers if it chose to erect signs itself and members asked me to get prices. By the next meeting I had obtained what seemed to be an exceptionally reasonable quote from a leading supplier of metal signs and I was instructed to go ahead and order two, one for each end of the terrace which I did. It was only when I was getting books and correspondence together to hand over to the new Clerk that I realised that the price I had been quoted was not per sign but per letter! (Count them!) In fairness to them, none of the Councillors ever complained to me and in fairness to me, the last time I passed the signs were still there so over the many years in between they were probably a bargain.

18: *SAILORS AND SHOWMEN*

The Town Clerk's job was becoming pretty much routine and I was able to gently update some of the procedures in the office and at meetings. I also benefited by getting to know my Pembroke Councillors. My first Mayor Brian Phillips, a past Mayor Joe Gough and a soon to be Mayor Ernie Morgan were particularly helpful during my learning process. I also found out who were the duds and who had useful knowledge or attributes. A good one to have on your side was Dillwyn Davies, a teacher and long-time Councillor, who had a particular skill in debates. He would stay silent but interested until the debate was about to run out of steam and then at just the right moment come in with a piece of information or experience from the past most eloquently delivered which almost invariably would swing the decision the way he wanted. I always called him, 'The Oracle'.

What wasn't routine was the number of events Haidee and I were being invited to as Mr & Mrs Town Clerk normally accompanying the Mayor & Mayoress. As well as reciprocal invitations such as Tenby Town Council to the Civic Ball at the De Valence Pavilion there was Luncheon with the Queen's Harbour Master at Pembroke Dock, the Annual Cocktail Party at the Officers Mess, Merrion Barracks, Castlemartin Royal Armoured Corps Range and Farewell Drinks with the German Liaison Officer at Castlemartin at the end of the Panzer training season. Very much a men only event however was the Pembrokeshire Life Offices Annual Luncheon at the Queen's Function Centre, Haverfordwest. This lunch was given by and for representatives of the nineteen insurance companies that had offices locally and their guests and I seem to recall the only women present being the waitresses. A one-off in 1983 was an invitation to Pembroke Power Station when they were presented with the Hinton Cup for being the power station displaying the best housekeeping in the workplace that year. This included a very interesting tour of the station followed by an excellent lunch. One event held in a pub was memorable for one reason only. While circulating, I found myself in a three way conversation with my two former bosses – Dillwyn Miles, Herald Bard and J Ronald Jones, by now retired Chief Constable with both of them claiming that, 'My boy done good'!

Talking of the Panzer Regiments training at Castlemartin every year, as each regiment came in the Commanding Officer would call to pay his respects to the Mayor. I would pour the drinks in the Mayor's Parlour and small wooden plaques with our coat of arms would be exchanged for a similar plaque with the regiment's insignia. Quite a collection built up on the walls of the parlour. One thing that did take a bit of getting used to was seeing German military uniforms at the annual Remembrance Day ceremonies. Other military invitations were at what was then RAF Brawdy. It was great to be in the VIP enclosure at the annual Air Day when the Hawks of the Red Arrows seemed to be performing just for you – which in a way they were because the focus of their display would be the VIP area.

The other events at Brawdy were Change of Command Ceremonies in 1980 and 1983 at USNAVFAC Brawdy – translation United States Navy Facility (Oceanographic Systems Atlantic) – real translation US Navy facility for watching and listening to Russian submarines. The ceremonies were held in the very large Hangar 3 at Brawdy. There was all the usual military pomp and ceremony, speeches and the rather incongruous sight of US sailors doing some really fancy marching to the music of a very British Royal Marine band. All good fun and an excellent buffet afterwards.

The invitation to beat them all and memorable in so many different ways was our visit to HMS Pembroke. In 1981 the Commanding Officer of HMS Pembroke, Captain P.T.'Paddy' Sheehan invited the Mayor and party from Pembroke Town Council to visit his shore base at Chatham. Sorting out the details was left to me and (in fairness mostly) to Lt. Andy Forsyth who, whatever his real job was, had been additionally lumbered with the grand title, 'Lieutenant For Welsh Affairs'. The visit would take place on 13th-14th October and the party would comprise the Mayor Charlie Thomas and his wife who was also his Mayoress, me and my wife Haidee together with Cllr. Ricky Sabido and his wife – I think the Deputy Mayor was unavailable. The Commander's Temporary Memorandum that gave all details of the visit and stated that Andy Forsyth would 'accompany the party throughout the visit' but fortunately he did get to sleep on his own.

As there was a security exercise at Chatham on the day of our arrival, we were asked not to arrive until 5.30pm and with no M25 in those days this meant a route, basically through London at around rush hour. Not the best time for the clutch to start to go on your car. The Thomas's and Sabido's were travelling together with Haidee and myself going separately in my car. We were some distance from Chatham when the clutch started playing up and it became more and more difficult to change gear just as the traffic got heavier and there was more and more need to do so. We only just made it and I was really pleased to see the main gates of the dockyard and even more pleased that the Captain's house was not too far inside. As soon as I decently could I explained my car problem and asked the Captain whether there was a garage locally he could suggest. After a quiet conversation with his Petty Officer Steward he came back to me and told me to just give the keys to his PO who would sort things out

The next item on the agenda was afternoon tea with the Captain's wife. Cups, saucers and plates had already been laid and there were cakes a plenty. The POSTD came in with the teapot and hot water jug on a silver salver, placed it on the table and was hovering obviously waiting for the Captain's wife to ask him to pour or to tell him that she would pour herself.

Captain Paddy Sheehan welcomes his guests

However, before any such decision could be made, the Mayor's wife grabbed the teapot and said, 'Shall I be Mother.' The look on the PO's face was worth a thousand words but the captain's wife, to her eternal credit, just smiled sweetly and said, 'Of course Mrs Thomas.'

Time to unpack and get ready for the evening meal – Supper 7.30pm for 8.00pm. I can't remember what we had just that it was fantastic and certainly far grander than anything my Mum would have called supper. I wasn't much of a wine drinker in those days but I do remember thinking that the wine was almost certainly one that I would never be able to afford. The PO Steward was very much in charge acting more and more like a butler supervising a team of trainee stewards serving table and another team of trainee cooks in the kitchen. The trainees seemed a bit nervous having to perform in the Captain's house and presence but they needn't have worried, they were superb.

After an excellent breakfast with the PO still in charge we were ready to start our tour at 9.15am. There was no sign of my car so I assumed it was at a local garage being sorted, was pleased about this but also pleased that I had brought my business chequebook with me with its overdraft facility. Our first stop was the imaginatively named No.1 Building for a presentation by the Captain and his staff about the work of HMS Pembroke followed by official photographs outside the Captain's Door – typical RN, there was a door that only the Captain and his guests could use.

There followed a very busy but fascinating morning visiting the Education Centre, Stewards School (where we had coffee), Cookery School, Gymnasium and Swimming Pool, SAFAB (had to look that up – it's Sailors and Families Advice Bureau), Galley, WRNS Quarters, and the Cash Clothing Store. It was during the morning that we learned that HMS Pembroke had been responsible for making Prince Charles and Diana's wedding cake and in typical Navy style had made two identical cakes which travelled to the venue in separate vehicles in very much the heir and a spare principle. At 12.20pm precisely we took a short walk to the Wardroom for what was described as 'Drinks followed by Top Table Lunch for 16'. Again I was too busy enjoying it to remember what we actually had to eat – just excellent.

The Cake

Obviously there was no rush as it was around 2.15pm before we departed by mini-bus for a tour of Chatham Dockyard which again was really fascinating especially the rope walk but the highlight for me was going aboard *HMS Dreadnought*, the Navy's first ever nuclear powered submarine. *Dreadnought* had been taken out of service earlier that year and was towed into dry dock at Chatham. She was later taken to Rosyth RN Dockyard where at the time of writing she still is – nuclear fuel and weapons removed but otherwise pretty much intact. There is a hope that she will be returned to Barrow-in-Furness where she was built once finally de-commissioned.

We returned to the Captain's house for final farewells and there was my car, gleaming with a full valet inside and out, a new clutch and a full service. I asked Paddy Sheehan how much I owed and he replied. 'Oh no. It's on the Navy. My PO has your keys and please do not embarrass him by offering him a tip.' Apparently their own workshop had done the work and I can't help thinking that they couldn't have had too many *Opel* clutches in stock. Then just to literally put icing on the cake, we were all presented with a little gift box containing a slice of Charles & Diana's (spare) wedding cake. We kept it for a while to show to everyone but eventually ate it and as with everything else naval, it was superb.

Unfortunately Paddy Sheehan was the last Captain of HMS Pembroke at Chatham when he was 'hauled out' by officers and ratings just over two years later on 29 October 1983. A closure party was there until February 1984 when the final connection with the Navy was severed. Part of the dockyard is open to the public as a museum well worth visiting but much of what was HMS Pembroke now houses a university. However, HMS Pembroke is not dead, the name is now carried by a Sandown

Class Minehunter commissioned in 1997. It would be great if the Town Council has renewed a link but I don't think that this is the case.

It wasn't all fun or all routine. There had been Hereditary Freemen of the Borough of Pembroke for centuries and the power and responsibility for the admission of new Freemen was a matter for the Borough Council. When that council was scrapped, the government for some unfathomable reason decided that this responsibility should be passed to South Pembrokeshire District Council. That council almost immediately realised how perverse this was and used Section 101 of the Local Government Act 1972 to formally delegate the power and responsibility to Pembroke Town Council. That council obviously recognising the importance of the matter almost immediately used that same Section of the Act to delegate the power and responsibility to its Town Clerk.

There were absolutely no benefits to being a Freeman other than being able to tell people that you were one. The tradition was that the first son of a Freeman could apply to also become a Freeman himself and I dealt with just a handful of applications in a year. All this entailed was to check the applicants details and Birth Certificate against the Register of Freemen. If all was in order, a fairly fancy certificate was signed by the Mayor and myself and that was that. Sometimes it was arranged that the Mayor would hand over the certificate so that photographs could be taken but more often than not it was just sent out by post. So centuries of tradition trundled on but this was the 1980s so I suppose it was bound to happen – I received an application from a daughter!

The solemn moment as sailors haul down the White Ensign for the last time at H.M.S. Pembroke. CL/45/29

I think my original reply was along the lines of 'that's not how it works' whereupon she went fairly ballistic and I knew that I would have to refer the matter to Council. I could give the Council no guidance as I was unable to find any precedents and as far as I could ascertain through local enquiries of Haverfordwest, etc. and more widely through the National Association of Local Councils, this 'problem' had not arisen anywhere else. Councillors were pretty much divided between '

You can't mess with centuries of tradition', 'We'll end up with daughters of daughters and hundreds of them' and 'Perhaps women should be allowed in' or 'We don't want to get sued'. The press got very much involved and I was interviewed on BBC Radio Wales trying desperately to sit on the fence. As decision day loomed we were unexpectedly saved when a legal ruling from on high said that admission of Freeman was not a power that the District Council was able to delegate. I tried to keep the smile off my face as I handed all the files and registers over to SPDC. Female Freemen were later admitted and I was told I had a good voice for radio – better I suppose than having a good face for it.

Time for more fun – this time all the fun of the fair. Another event in Pembroke steeped in tradition and ceremonial was the annual Michaelmas Fair. This dated back to medieval times when it was a hiring fair for agricultural labourers, etc. but was now just a funfair. It always opened on the second Thursday in October and operated for three days almost totally blocking Main Street for much of five days with the road being completely closed to traffic for set-up on the Wednesday afternoon, for the fair itself on Thursday and Friday evenings and Saturday afternoon and evening and for break-down on Sunday morning until 10.30am.

The opening was performed by the Mayor accompanied by the two Macebearers and the Town Crier who opened proceedings with The Cry Of The Fair. Once the Town Crier had made the proclamation, the Mayor made a short speech to declare the fair open using one of the fair rides as their platform and then would follow a tradition dating not quite back to medieval times by taking the first ride in the dodgem cars followed by most of the Councillors. Then the party would retire to the Town Hall leaving the general public to enjoy themselves and the ride operators and stallholders to sell their wares and merchandise. I don't recall ever seeing any cattle though.

THE CRY OF THE PEMBROKE FAIR

Oyez, Oyez, the Mayor of the Town of Pembroke doth in Her Majesty's name strictly charge and command all manner of persons coming or resorting to this Fair that they and every one of them do keep Her Majesty's peace.

It is further charged and commanded in Her Majesty's name that all manner of persons coming or resorting to this Fair that they shall not presume to bear, carry or wear any manner of weapon whatsoever except the Mayor of the Town of Pembroke and his Officers, the Sheriff of the County of Pembroke and his Ministers, the Justices of the Peace and their Attendants on pain of forfeiture of all such armour or weapon so worn or borne to the contrary and his or their bodies to be imprisoned.

And it is further charged and commanded in Her Majesty's name that all manner of persons coming or resorting to this Fair and bringing with them any kind of wares or merchandise made and provided upon pain of forfeiture of all such wares or whatsoever that they use true weights and measures in the sale thereof according to the Statute of Winchester in that case merchandise bought or sold to the contrary and his or their bodies to be imprisoned.

It is further charged and commanded in Her Majesty's name that all manner of persons coming or resorting to this Fair and bringing with them any kind of Cattle whatsoever that they cause the buyers' and sellers' names of all such kinds of Cattle bought or sold to be entered into the Tolls or Bailiffs' Book of the saidTown of Pembroke and pay or cause to be paid all such Tolls or Fees as are due or have been accustomarily paid on all such kinds of Cattle bought or sold to the contrary and his or their bodies to be imprisoned.

And for the deciding of all matters of difference that shall arise in the buying or selling of any kinds of wares, merchandise or Cattle whatsoever the Mayor of the Town of Pembroke will keep a Court of Pied Poundre where the persons grieved shall be righted according to Law

This Fair holds Three days.   God Save The Queen

I usually decided not to exercise my right to carry a weapon.

The Town Hall was the venue for a reception hosted by the South West Section of The Showmen's Guild of Great Britain. This too had become a tradition with invitations going to all Councillors and spouses, various local dignitaries, Mayors from other Pembrokeshire towns and (the excuse for it all) residents and business people from Main Street who were adversely affected by the road closure and general noise of the fair. It was my job to arrange caterers to supply and serve a light buffet and to obtain a plentiful supply of drinks. The whole tab was always picked up without question by the Showmen's Guild and the only instruction I ever received from them was in effect, 'Don't bother with wine and never run out of drink'.

After my first such event and seeing how things worked, I was able to combine my two jobs for the first time, co-ordinating the event and liaising with the Showmen's Guild as Town Clerk and supplying the booze as Landlord of the Brook. The numbers invited were relatively small and some just stayed for the buffet and perhaps one drink which made the total consumed even more impressive. For the 1980 reception, I supplied the following:-

      7 Bottles of Scotch Whisky, 3 of Gin and 1 of Vodka

      3 Bottles of Sherry and 1 of *Cinzano*

      9 Bottles of lemonade, 2 of cordial and 1 soda syphon

      60 Bottles of mixers and 12 of *Pepsi* Cola

      48 Bottles of *Worthington E*

Everything was supplied on sale or return so this is what was actually consumed and it was perhaps unsurprising that a number of very prim and proper ladies of a certain age became very much less so and some very sober men became totally legless. One of my Mayors who shall be nameless fell down the stairs on leaving and had to be carried to his car which thankfully someone else was driving. I am informed that this great tradition has been maintained and a very reliable source was present not many years ago when a certain Mayor of Haverfordwest became so drunk that when he wandered out to have another look at the fair the Town Hall door was locked on him so that he couldn't get back in. Over the years I got on very well with the showmen and was told that I had been made an honorary member of the Guild but I don't think this was ever official.

Another thing that I hoped would be a source of fun and interest was Twinning but this did not materialise. I knew that other places with Twin Towns often enjoyed very good, enjoyable and interesting exchange visits. Contrary to popular belief, at Town and Parish level this was almost invariably at the participants own expense rather than the taxpayer. The same could not be said for some of the junkets at District and County level.

Pembroke still maintains the tradition

Pembroke had twinned in 1977 with Bergen in Germany but the Twinning Association did not seem particularly active and Council seemed to keep twinning very much at arms length.

Perhaps I found the answer when I discovered that Bergen's full name was in fact Bergen-Belsen. (Don't mention the War!) Still. I did get a Christmas card every year from the Stadt Direktor (Town Clerk) and I still have hanging in my hallway a nice little souvenir barometer which fortunately just reads, 'Bergen'.

19: *A FEW MORE ROUNDS*

I have mentioned us taking separate holidays from the Brook and very often other time off would be in the same category or would not really be time off at all. We both played 'away' games with our respective darts teams which was fine but not really 'off duty'. We would sometimes, very rarely, take a couple of hours off together in the evening but invariable would go to another pub and before long would be checking out their prices, customers, food trade, etc. so again not really off duty. In the early days we would go to Haverfordwest Licensed Victuallers Association functions which were very much still work related. Sometimes we would be invited to functions as Mr & Mrs Pembroke Town Clerk but again that very often felt like work. I would be away from the pub for evening Council meetings, but again that would be work.

I know we had a 'break' in the afternoons but frequently one of us would be going to the cash and carry or bank and the other would be doing jobs around the pub that could only be done when it was closed. We did get to take a few trips around Pembrokeshire taking Mum & Dad out and about but in fairness, Haidee very often took them on her own. There were a few good breaks together when we could really switch off and enjoy ourselves and one of these was when I got a letter from Beryl Dando, Secretary of Dale Carnival Committee inviting us both to act as judges at the August Carnival. She also invited the Brook to enter a tug-of-war team to compete for the *George Jackson Cup* (I had donated a trophy when I left the village but I honestly had no part in naming it!). It was a really lovely day 'back home' and we thoroughly enjoyed it. I'm pretty sure the Brook entered a team but I can't remember who I presented the cup to.

Really though the one true (part) day off was Christmas Day. Our first Christmas Day set the pattern that would become a tradition. We opened from 11am to 1pm only and I tried to make it as much as possible like the Christmas Day lunchtimes I remembered in the pub at home when I was (nearly) old enough to drink. Then everyone would have a good time but all would leave, often with many 'carry-outs', to be home in good time for Christmas Dinner (It was lunch but we always called it dinner). At the Brook, no bar food was served (except a microwaved *Bowyers* pie or pasty for anyone who had missed breakfast) and I bought every regular (or even occasional) customer their first drink, kept things as 'jolly' as possible but made sure everyone was gone by 1.30pm at the latest ready for our Dinner to be served in the lounge bar.

Haidee, with help from Mum would then serve up to the multitude from the kitchen which opened directly into the lounge bar and had the benefit of two large cookers. Present over the years were myself and Haidee. Sons Bill & Douglas, Mother Betty & Father George, my brother Nigel and our caravan 'lodger' Horst Vietze. At least one year we were joined by my sister Maggie, husband Phil and children Chris & Libby and also at least once by my Mother-in-law June Coupe. Sister Jennifer and a selection of her six children could also be there. I think the record number was well into the teens. The adults had the benefit of self-service of any tipple they fancied from the bar and the kids thought they had died and gone to Heaven when they were given the run of the public bar (not behind it) with weak shandies, playing cards, dominoes and games, the light on the dartboard and endless free plays on the juke box – their own real pub. At some stage in the proceedings, I would make what became a traditional appearance in fancy dress, usually as the Christmas Fairy holding a police truncheon with a silver star attached as my wand. That one real night off a year was great

Talking of buying drinks, the problem of 'putting one in' was one I was quite proud of solving. Very often a customer would wish to buy someone else a drink but they would have a fairly full glass, not be ready for another and would say 'Put one in for me'. The drink would be paid for leaving bar staff with the problem of remembering who had got what 'in' and whether they had had it yet and the customer with the problem of remembering whether or not he had got one 'in'. Everybody did their best to keep a record in their head or on scraps of paper but there were one or two customers who would claim their 'one in' more than once and others who would forget unless reminded. In a flash of inspiration the answer came to me one day to be some form of token. I acquired a quantity of steel discs about 3.5cm in diameter stamped with a letter 'B' which entitled the bearer to one of what they normally drank. I forget where I got them from. They certainly worked well, in fact better than well as in addition to no more arguments, many discs were never redeemed and I had to have more made. They also gave enormous pleasure to a few who saved them up so that they could drink a whole evening 'free' from time to time.

Every year in season we would have the pleasure of the company of numbers of baby frogs, a plague that became much more noticeable after an irrigation pond was dug in the field behind my parents' bungalow in Brookside. Mum didn't like them at all and would insist on the front door step being swept before she opened the door in case any came in but some always seemed to gain access. A few also made it as far as the Brook and from time to time someone would pick up a little frog on the way in and deposit it in a mate's glass as soon as they weren't looking. Quite amusing, if it wasn't your glass, to see it doing a perfect breast stroke in the head of a pint. The frog would be scooped out, often to be put in another person's glass before eventual release back to the wild. I don't think anyone ever actually swallowed a frog but I do remember one particular frog fatality. As it was being scooped out of a glass, it hopped out of a hand and fell to the floor where someone accidentally stepped on it. This prompted one of those spontaneous acts of group lunacy which made pubs so great – the frog had to be given a decent funeral. Numerous volunteers set to work and using empty cigarette packets, matchboxes, cocktail sticks and anything else available fashioned a lovely boat aboard which the deceased froglet was gently placed. Virtually everyone in the bar then went outside to watch as the boat was carefully launched into the brook that gave the Brook Inn it's name, was set alight and sailed away into the distance for the perfect Viking funeral.

Another memorable incident involved a somewhat larger animal – a big kitten or small cat owned by Mrs Austin who lived in a cottage almost opposite the Brook near the entrance to Brookside. Mrs Austin was universally known as 'The Spanish Lady' not because she was Spanish but because she had taught Spanish dancing and always took part in the village Carnival wearing full Flamenco costume. Her feline somehow managed to get itself trapped in a drain just outside our bar door. The Spanish Lady was in a panic and ever-helpful, Horst Vietze went to see what he could do with the assistance of several spectators. It was soon obvious that the drain cover would have to be lifted to release the cat and a lot of earth and debris would have to be moved to release the drain cover.

Veetsie borrowed my pick-axe and set to work. After some strenuous digging, hacking and prising and considerable shedding of sweat, the drain cover was finally freed and the cat lifted out. One of the onlookers who had obviously always wanted to be a Vet volunteered to check the cat out and Mrs

Austin rushed into the bar and came out with a glass of brandy. Everyone present, especially Veetsie, thought that this was his reward for all the digging he had done but no, the Spanish Lady proceeded to dip her finger in it and feed it to her cat. Poor old Veetsie was speechless but she did say thank you later.

Now for something a bit more alien (perhaps). The Ladies Darts team had been playing an away game and were returning to the Brook with two cars in convoy and passengers including my mother and my wife. The lead car was being driven by my sister-in-law to be, Janice Roberts who had not had an alcoholic drink as she was driving. She describes the incident as follows:-

'We hadn't gone far out of Milford when there was a large VERY bright light almost above us. First of all we thought it was the rescue helicopter out of Brawdy with its search beam on and it sort of went side by side with us along the road, possibly about 50 yards to the right of us over the hedge, as much as 150ft up which was too low for the helicopter. This went on for at least five minutes when all of a sudden it took off at such a really fast speed, still going in the same direction with the light still on'.

'We got to the Burgage Green turning into 'Tish (There'd been no sign of a light once we got out of the Sandy Hill dip), we had passed Castle Cottages, the pair of semi-detached cottages on the left, when this bright light suddenly appeared just above the hedge by the side of me. Perfectly round like someone shining a light, not so high this time. I slowed right down and opened the window to hear the helicopter (as we thought) but <u>there was no noise at all</u>. It was foot down and in through the Brook door as fast as we could go. I have absolutely no explanation for it. The light was exceptionally bright and we felt that a helicopter couldn't have taken off at the speed that this 'thing' did. We were all quite spooked by it. The next day, someone, I can't remember who, went to the last sighting place to see if it was a weather balloon but nothing was found and apparently no weather balloons were up in that area at the time.'

I remember that everyone involved genuinely believed that they had seen something that they were totally unable to explain. Another UFO incident, which probably took place after the one so graphically described above by Janice, was somewhat easier to explain. I think that again it was a Ladies Darts night when Mum decided that it was time for her to walk home the short but very dark distance to her bungalow in Brookside. In no time at all, she burst back through the door saying that there was a strange stationery red light between her and home. She set out again, this time with an escort who eventually established that there was indeed a light shining quite brightly and totally still. Closer examination showed that it wasn't from outer space but from the dashboard of Graham Sutton's *JCB*.

There were other things that moved in mysterious ways at night. On a number of occasions during our time at the Brook our regular customers would be joined by a group of strangers who were all very smartly dressed, very well behaved young men usually accompanied by one who was perhaps slightly older and fairly obviously in charge. For example, he would decide when they left and how many drinks they had but all very discreetly done and always with polite thanks to the Landlord. They all came from Hereford – they were all SAS.

They would be relaxing before a night exercise which would normally involve 'attacking' one of the Milford Haven oil refineries. Their approach could be from land or sea but was always on the basis of silent infiltration. One of the security guards at the *Amoco* refinery once told me that they would often be told that the SAS were coming at sometime in the next few nights and would increase patrols and vigilance. They would invariably never see or hear a thing until they opened a locked door or desk drawer and found a note saying, 'Bang – you're dead' or something similar.

I have mentioned regular customers earlier but there were also some who could perhaps be categorised as regular occasionals. Some we knew from our time in Dale, some who I knew from playing darts against them and some whose first allegiance was to other drinking establishments such as the Sports & Social Club in the village but who still called in at the Brook and some who maybe just didn't go out for a drink very regularly. Among these were the Gainfort clan. Dai Gainfort had been a good mate when we were in Dale and his brothers Ron and Kenny I also knew well. Brother Dennis lived in St Ishmaels with his wife Yvonne. Dennis suffered a stroke at a very young age but still enjoyed a pint. Graham Sutton who built all the bungalows in Brookside including Mum and Dad's was always helpful and Terry Jenkins who worked for him was another customer.

Bob Edwards was a coastguard in Dale and gave me his collection of Royal Navy cap tallies which I framed and displayed in the pub. His wife Margaret died very young and very quickly from cancer. Another coastguard was Sid Johnson who was from the west of England. Malcolm Orton was quiet spoken and friendly and his wife Hilary was an artist. Mum bought one of her local landscapes which I still have on my wall, Brothers Mike and Glyn Pawlett were both from Tish. Glyn's son Jonny recently ran the Brook for five years with his partner Sally Llewellin. Glyn was famous for a story about him using the wrong door for a toilet visit in the night and getting locked outside his house in the nude. Donna Jenkins was more of a regular and probably our youngest. She was always good for a laugh and I remember one occasion when she complained how few crisps there were in the packet she had just bought. I banged my hand down on it and said, 'There's a lot more now'. I did give her another packet eventually.

Another occasional customer was Paul Jenkins who, if he visited, always sat up at the bar where he demonstrated a remarkable talent. Where some people were said to make every other word a swear word, Paul could far exceed that and used every possible grammatical form of the F-word. For example, if an item inconveniently and unfortunately was broken, it would be,'The f***ing f***er's f***ing f***ed'. Luckily he was quietly spoken and everything was said in a conversational tone so he was only ever asked to tone it down if someone who didn't know him was close by. It was just the way he spoke and he almost certainly had no idea that he was doing it most of the time.

Paul was known as a drug user and unfortunately also as a very small-time supplier and had minor convictions for both possession and supply but was always totally clean and straight when he used our pub. Two similar stories circulated about Paul both of which could be true. He lived in a caravan in the village and it was certainly a fact that he grew his own cannabis in and around his garden and attached black plastic bags to his fence to shield it from view. One story is that a neighbour looked over the fence and remarked how well his tomato plants were coming on and the other is that he had cannabis growing in a greenhouse somewhere and asked someone to keep them watered while he was away for a few days which she did all the time convinced that they were actually tomatoes. Police were under no such illusions when they made a number of raids.

In the latter half of 1983, nobody was more surprised than the police who arrested him to find that Paul Jenkins had been a fairly major player in an international conspiracy to import controlled drugs into the country. The drugs had been brought in to a secluded cove in North Pembrokeshire near Newport where a large waterproof storage compartment big enough to stand up and walk around in had been constructed from timber and fibreglass UNDER the beach. Some of the leading members of the gang were already in custody and this seemed way out of Paul's league but Jenkins was a skilled mechanic especially with outboard motors and diesel engines and he had been recruited to play the key role of keeping the gang's fleet of six boats seaworthy. He had also collected a car from France and had constructed secret compartments in cars to conceal drugs.

When he was interviewed by Det. Sgt. Alan Coles (who had been a Detective Constable in Milford Haven during my time there), Jenkins, who was aged 35 at the time, fairly readily admitted his involvement and estimated that three tons of cannabis with a street value of £6 million had been brought to Pembrokeshire. He was the only local man involved. At Swansea Crown Court in July 1984 Soren Berg-Arnbak from Denmark was sentenced to 8 years imprisonment and deportation and the other ringleader Englishman Robin Boswell was sentenced to 10 years, and fined £75k with £75k costs. He also faced a £1.3 million bill from Inland Revenue. Kenneth Dewar and his son Kash Dewar received 5 years each and three others including Boswell's wife received lesser sentences.

Paul Jenkins pleaded Guilty and was sentenced to 6 years in prison and to pay £2k towards the Legal Aid Fund. He returned to St Ishmaels on serving his sentence and later married. In February 1985 the last member of the team was finally brought to justice when David Walter Frijs a South African living in France was sentenced to two and a half years for conspiracy to import controlled drugs. The case was the subject of a BBC TV documentary and was detailed in the book *Operation Seal Bay* by Pat Molloy the former Head of Dyfed-Powys CID. In his book Molloy says that Jenkins was recruited by the Dewars who he had first met in the 1970s when they were visiting a woman who lived in a cottage at St Anns which Paul used to visit to smoke pot. The cottage was on my 'patch' and was actually at Kete. I also visited fairly frequently, not in the evening to smoke pot but on patrol in the daytime to drink real coffee served in a bowl, to chat, listen to gossip, collect car registration numbers and waste my time as CID weren't at all interested then.

A view of the store built under the beach

Occasionally, I would be asked to provide a bar away from the pub for an event or special occasion. My first job would be to apply to the Magistrates for what was very appropriately called an Occasional Licence. Only three come to mind, the first being for an auction held at Sandy Hill Farm which was not particularly remarkable other than being a welcome source of additional income. The second was for an eighteenth birthday party at a farm in St Ishmaels. I drove up in the afternoon in the Brook van with stock, etc. and son Bill to get things set up. We agreed a location with the farmer and we were told that there were some building blocks available from which we could make a bar to serve from. I envisaged breeze blocks and left Bill to carry on building while I returned to the Brook for more stock and other bits and pieces. I came back much later, just before our planned opening time to find the bar just about completed and Bill totally exhausted. It turned out that the 'breeze blocks' were actually solid concrete blocks much bigger and several times heavier than I had imagined which he had carried a considerable distance on his own. I took pity and after the initial rush I let him go off and join the birthday girl (Joanna I think) and her guests many of which were his friends in any event.

The most memorable by far was in July 1981 for a celebration of the wedding of Prince Charles and Diana. The event – a glorified fete, was to be held in the grounds of St Ishmaels School and I was asked to provide a bar. I successfully applied for an Occasional Licence, bought a large supply of plastic glasses and ordered in fairly considerable extra dry and wet stock. I couldn't serve my best selling *Worthington BB* as it wouldn't travel well so I got in a good supply of *Double Diamond* in kegs and my usual *Harp* lager. I agreed the best location and arranged an electricity supply for the coolers with Headmaster Bill Roberts. Then at almost literally the last minute – I think the day before, Bill was told that the Education Committee would not permit the sale of alcohol within the school grounds. No bar could be allowed and I was lumbered with loads of unwanted stock. But this was St Ishmaels and no-one up in County Hall was going to spoil its party. Within hours a solution was found and agreed (by all concerned in Tish) – a section of fence was removed, my bar would be very slightly re-located into farmer John Llewellin's field with the front of the bar taking the place of the fence section. There were no sales of alcohol within school grounds but no obstacle whatsoever to alcohol being passed into the school grounds after it had been purchased in the field. The plastic glasses also proved to be a very good investment. The half-pint and spirit sizes were very robust and could be collected, washed and re-used in future. Even better, the oversized pint size proved to be not robust and unless held very carefully could squidge up shedding some contents or even split shedding all the liquid which no doubt added to my already very healthy takings.

20: *FIRE AND SNOW*

By 30th August 1983, my brother Nigel had bought his own home in Neyland and his wife-to-be Janice Roberts was living in Milford Haven. On that night they had enjoyed an evening with us at the Brook and were travelling home together with Derek who was Nigel's colleague and at that time lodger. Janice was driving and had decided to take the short cut via Rickeston and Thornton when Nigel and Derek decided that nature called so Janice stopped to let them enter a gateway at the side of the road. They were still near the gate when a sheet of flame erupted in front of them. Fortunately they had both done up their zips as the next thing to hit them was a blast of heat enough to singe eyebrows and the hairs on Derek's arm. This was the fire at the *Amoco* refinery caused by a 'boil-over' that burned for two days before 70 appliances and 150 firefighters finally put it out. The following night, the glow in the sky was still clearly visible from St Ishmaels which according to Nigel was a much better location to view it from.

Amoco cooled down a bit. Fire covered 4 acres at height

Nigel remembers another occasion when he came to the Brook for a darts match with a number of his workmates from WSC (Worthington Service Corporation) in Thornton – I think that was its name then, it's had numerous name changes, take-overs and location changes during his career with the company up to his retirement and Worthington was nothing to do with beer, their business was high-tech pumps and water treatment equipment. Anyway, back to the story – one of his workmates drove back home to Templeton after the darts. In the early hours of the morning, his wife woke up feeling very cold. Her husband was snoring alongside her but she noticed that the bedroom door was open. She got up to close it and noticed that the kitchen light was still on. Going to turn the kitchen light off she noticed that the back door was wide open. Before closing the back door she realised that the car was not in the drive. Going out to the road she found the car parked at the end of their cul-de-sac with the lights full on and the engine still running. Needless to say, he wasn't very popular with his wife for a while but St Ishmaels to Templeton via Haverfordwest without mishap in that condition was quite an achievement surely.

One fire much nearer home was at the Copper Coins or the Four Seasons Country Club as it became and I slept right through it. Frank and Mrs Dunn and their son Peter had decided to leave the Coins and had moved to a house overlooking the beach at St Brides. Frank then worked for Basil Jones Auctioneers including running the cafe at Haverfordwest Livestock Market. They had been good friends and neighbours and never competitors as very often their customers, especially those from Milford Haven and surrounds, often called in for a drink with us before moving on to the club bringing us trade we wouldn't otherwise have had.

It is at this point that my memory and the memories of my family fail, I cannot pin down when the Dunns left, when the club name was changed, when the fire took place, whether the club re-opened after the fire and what were the names of the new owners or where they moved to when they left. There was an older woman, very much the matriarch, a younger man, I think her son, who was called Rudi (short for Rudolph) and one other. They had enjoyed a major football pools win which probably financed their purchase and amazingly had another major win some time after that. The new owners were friendly enough and were never a problem to us. Son Bill remembers going to Discos there with his mates, dancing with the Matriarch and enjoying free drinks as a reward for this chore.

They also did their best to draw in the crowds by booking only slightly faded stars including Alvin Stardust and Joe Brown (not sure whether with or without his Bruvvers). For some time they also employed a very good chef called Tom who became one of our lunchtime regulars. Tom had worked at the Royal Navy College, Greenwich and his speciality was jugged hare samples of which and other treats he would sometimes bring in for Haidee (I usually got a taste later).

Anyway, back to the fire. As I said, I slept through every minute of it despite the fire engine re-filling with water from the hydrant virtually underneath my bedroom window. Haidee, Bill and Douglas were of course wide awake and followed proceedings throughout and Bill remembers climbing up onto the flat roof above our kitchen to get a better view. The Copper Coins had originally been built by Morris Allen who had followed Gladys Hughes/Dillon as landlord of the Brook Inn and who had carried out much of the renovation, changes and 'improvements' to what was now our pub. When I eventually walked up to look at the damage to the Coins the following morning (after getting over my strop because no-one had bothered to wake me up), I saw clear evidence of the same huge skill, loving care and attention to detail that he had employed at the Brook. From what was left of the Copper Coins large flat roof I could see that the whole thing had been constructed from old army ammunition boxes!

After all the excitement had died down, I remembered that the day before the fire a complete stranger had come into the Brook for just a couple of drinks. When I served him my ex-copper's hairs stood up on my neck and I couldn't help noticing his 'prison tan' (the pallor of someone who has not seen the sun for a considerable time) and I just wondered! The Matriarch, Rudi, et al moved back to England. I can't remember where but it was to a pub somewhere and we were invited to visit but never did. When I was writing this, I *googled* Fours Seasons Country Club and the only thing to come up was in Portugal in the Algarve:- *The Four Seasons Country Club founded 1986!* and I just wondered!

During the evening of Thursday January 7th 1982, it started to snow. It never snows in Pembrokeshire so it would soon stop and would be melted away by morning but it didn't and it wasn't. Janice Roberts who was living at Bicton cottage at the time, was at the Brook when the snow started. She tried to drive home but totally failed to get her car up the slope that was Trewarren Road, brought the car back to the Brook and walked. By the time she finally made the fair distance home, her overcoat was coated with snow and literally frozen solid.

This was the start of the famous Blizzard of '82 which covered virtually all of Wales and where for the most part it snowed continuously for 36 hours. Our part of Pembrokeshire had almost certainly not had the depth of snow that had fallen in other parts of the Principality but the blizzard conditions had blown snow off the fields and trapped it between the banks and hedges of all the roads. In common with many other villages, St Ishmaels was totally cut off. The next thing to happen was the total loss of the village's electricity supply and it stayed off for SEVEN days. At the Brook we were lucky in many ways but most importantly I had only just had a major delivery from James Williams stocking up on everything after the busy Christmas period. One of our two large cookers in the kitchen ran on *Calor Gas* and our exterior gas tanks had recently been topped up. We had an open coal fire and a good supply of fuel and also had *Calor Gas* heaters.

When we moved in there had been an elderly back-up generator included in the ingoing inventory but I had never managed to start it or ever worked out how to connect it so I had sold it in our 'George Dodd's rubbish' auction. I had replaced it however with a large number of brand new hurricane lamps and had a plentiful supply of paraffin to fuel them and several boxes of candles so lighting was also well covered. The till could be worked manually and it was cold enough to get away without coolers for the beer. We also had two big cabinet freezers full of food and the bottle store where they were located was so cold that the loss of electricity was not really a great problem for much of those seven days and we didn't lose a great deal. Not everyone was so lucky, Judy John had a number of chickens in her freezer and decided to bury them in the snow outside her home. They didn't survive.

At first, things were fairly quiet but as word got round that not only were we open for business but also had light and heat, which many did not, we got busier and busier. Haidee was able to offer a fairly limited range of hot food and also had a couple of large cauldrons of home-made soup or broth permanently on the go which proved to be very popular. She was also able to respond to more unusual requests like warming milk for the baby's bottle. We began to see village residents who had never darkened our doors in the past and our regulars soon became accustomed to playing darts and dominoes by the light of hurricane lamps and got used to beer marginally warmer than usual and to harvesting ice for drinks from outdoors if required. The only facilities not on offer were the juke box and the bandit.

The next thing to happen was most of the telephones in the village going dead either through lines being down or batteries running low but fortunately for us both our land-line and public payphone kept on working throughout. As a result, as this fact became known, we almost became the communications centre for the village. An example of this was when a Lindsway Road resident broke a leg climbing over deep snow, Haidee was contacted by RAF Brawdy Air Sea Rescue and was asked to advise the family when the helicopter would be arriving and to choose a suitable landing area. She walked up with the boys and with the help of willing volunteers the victim was made ready and a large 'H' was marked out in a nearby field. Mission accomplished.

Another mercy mission at an earlier stage was when Mum and Dad realised that the village shop didn't stock the 'right' food for their obviously fussy cat. This resulted in my teenage niece Helen walking all the way from Neyland to Tish with a supply of cat food on a sled. Having arrived, she stayed with her grandparents for the duration. I knew nothing about this until after the mission had been completed otherwise I may well have suggested that any cat would eat anything if it was hungry enough. Arrangements were also made for human essentials with it being possible to collect milk from Read's farm and with bread being brought in by boat to Monkhaven by teacher Peter Sharpe.Most of the new customers we gained during that magic week disappeared as soon as the lights came back on but we did retain a few. I cashed literally dozens of cheques during that time, many with unfamiliar names signing them and I even took a number of five pound notes that had gone out of circulation in 1971! These were as new and beautifully flat – obviously straight from under the mattress and luckily the bank accepted them without any fuss. They say it's an ill wind that blows no-one any good and that wind certainly blew us some good. Not just in an exceptional weeks takings but also the surreal but enjoyable experience of it all.

But there was still more good to come. With the combination of a bit of a thaw and lots of work with locally owned tractors and *JCB*s it was eventually just about possible to get out of the village by road and I was on to my last cask of *Worthington BB*. I phoned James Williams and was told that there was no way they could deliver but if I could get there I could collect some beer from their yard in Haverfordwest. My little Brook van wasn't up to the job so I asked Graham Sutton if I could borrow his *Ford Transit* van and for such an essential purpose, he immediately agreed. I made it to the yard without too much trouble and I was loaded up with some lager and other odds and ends and I think five, maybe six 18 gallon kils of BB. As they did so the guys said that they didn't know how good it would be as it had been outside and had frozen solid. I got back safely with my valuable cargo and with only slight damage to Graham's shiny new *Transit* caused when my load shifted. (He was very good, he never ever mentioned it). The casks were loaded up on the stillage and the first one came into use after a day or so. I prided myself on keeping a good pint but some brews were better than others and this was fantastic. It was sparkling clear with a great head and excellent taste. The regulars noticed towith it being possible to collect milk from Read's farm and with bread being brought in by boat to Monkhaven by teacher Peter Sharpe. such an extent that as the days went on they kept asking how much more of that frozen beer I had left. Nowadays freezing is part of the brewing process for a number of beers and lagers and thanks to the internet I now know that freezing or 'jacking' beer and cider increases the alcohol content That's where Applejack gets its name. So no wonder they all liked it, not just bright, sparkling, clear and tasty but stronger as well.

Talking of cashing cheques, during my whole six years at the Brook, I never had one that 'bounced' but one, only one, cost me money. Dickie Bastin was new to the village and became a customer. He was ex-RAF where his last job had been maintaining helicopters in Guyana. He drove a very rare, unusual, expensive *Matra Simca* sports car. It was left-hand drive with the steering wheel offset to the right and very unusually had three individual front seats. Dickie had a large Husky type dog which always sat on the right seat and as they drove towards you it looked very much like the dog was driving – very disconcerting. Dickie got together with Lynda Thomas (sister of Dai, Adrian, Fay and Nicholas) and they left the village to run a bar in Gibraltar. On their break back in St Ishmaels they would call in at the Brook and on one occasion Dickie asked me to cash a cheque which I was happy to do but when I paid it into the business A/c I was charged a 'transaction fee' as it was drawn on a Gibraltar bank – not a problem. Dickie and Lynda obviously liked the Brook as they ran it for two years from 1997.

21: *TIME TO CALL TIME*

When we went into the Brook, we thought that a stay of five years would be about right. We had seen too many landlords and ladies over the years who had been in the job or in the same pub far too long, gone stale, lost trade and not really cared that they had lost it. Sometimes a change of scene would be the answer such as when Dennis and June Blackman moved from the Lobster Pot at Marloes to the Griffin Inn at Dale. Sometimes, in the words of *Monty Python* it would be time for something completely different but I had the advantage of already doing something completely different in Pembroke part of the time.

As we entered our sixth year however, a number of factors came into play. St Ishmaels Sports & Social Club had opened shiny new premises in November 1982 which were much more spacious, had far better facilities and were much more attractive to customers than their original building which had been basically a large wooden hut. People were no longer calling at the Brook for a couple of drinks before visiting the Copper Coins/Four Seasons. Although takings had risen very nicely year on year, net profits (i.e. our 'wages') had not risen by the same percentage due to increased costs. Pembrokeshire was attracting a different type of holidaymaker – still perhaps looking for a meal and one drink, less likely to visit for an evening drinking session and more likely to steal soap and toilet paper from the ladies loo. Strangely enough, we found that they were far less likely to steal a half-used loo roll or a bar of soap that had been cut in half.

Local regular trade was also dying a little – in some cases literally. Over the years we had lost Eddie Edwards and I had attended a packed Sandy Hill Chapel for the funeral of Arthur Bowen. The minister who conducted an excellent service became an occasional Brook customer but obviously couldn't make up for the loss of Arthur. There were several others but the one we possibly missed most, not for his purchases but for his company was Taff Davies who died early in 1982 after a fairly lengthy illness. We had a lovely letter from his son Reg thanking us for our kindness during his father's illness. I don't remember any particular acts of kindness but just enjoying the sense of humour he never lost. In his heyday, when he knew that holidaymakers were listening, he would engage in an apparently serious conversation with any fellow regular or whoever was behind the bar, who would obviously be in on the act, and talk about such things as how poor his crop of rice had been in his paddy field this year or how he had been advised to put salt down to deter slugs only to find when he crept out after dark to have a look that the slugs were dipping his lettuces in the salt before eating them.

I can't remember at what stage we decided to make our sixth year our last in the Brook Inn but obviously it made sense to take advantage of the summer trade before leaving so just before Midsummer Day (24th June) we gave notice of our intention to leave on 29th September 1983 (Michaelmas Day) exactly six years after we moved in. In the event, for some reason I can't remember, probably to help the new tenants with an accommodation problem, our last day of trading was 11th of September with the changeover being the following day. So we didn't quite make that six years.

Our decision having been made, the first priority was to find somewhere to live. We had initially held on to 77 Blue Anchor

Way, Dale and used it as a summer let but the letting agents didn't seem to expend a great deal of time or effort for their fees and we were never anything like fully booked. Even so, it was still a chore to supervise changeovers and undertake cleaning especially after one apparently respectable but particularly dirty family. In the end, we had put the house on the market and sold it to a couple from Birkenhead in 1981. It was quite a wrench as we had spent some very happy years there and it had been a wonderful place for the boys to enjoy their childhood.

As it happened, the housing problem solved itself. Mum and Dad had known that we wouldn't stay at the Brook for ever and felt that with their advancing years they would prefer to be nearer shops, doctors, dentists, bus services, etc. and had been looking for somewhere in or near Milford Haven. They found their ideal property at 2 Upper Hill Street, Hakin, a small terraced cottage literally next to the local shop, with a good sized but manageable secluded garden to the rear and panoramic views from the front over the harbour and docks which had begun their transformation to Milford Haven Marina. They had snapped the place up, knowing that it would sell quickly but were then for some time in a bridging loan situation.

Obvious solution – we would buy their bungalow at 5 Brookside. We obtained valuations from two estate agents and took the average which was £29,500 – not a bad return on their investment as they had paid Graham Sutton £12,950 for the land and new build bungalow with fitted carpets throughout in July 1974. They had only paid £19,500 for their Hakin cottage so even with the bridging loan costs, there would be a good bit over to supplement their pensions and we also agreed that if we sold the bungalow within two years, we would pay them one third of any profit. We saved a bit more money as our solicitor, Michael James of Haverfordwest was happy to act for both parties.The next area of concern was work. Pembroke Town Council had previously agreed to increase my hours as Town Clerk from 20 to 25 per week and I had already also taken on the (very) part time job of Secretary to the South Pembrokeshire Road Safety Committee. In 1981 I had got the job of Census Officer for Pembroke, being trained myself and then recruiting, training and finally supervising a fairly large number of enumerators to undertake the collection of census papers from Pembroke households. This particular job which had lasted about six months, wouldn't come round again for another ten years but I was confident that I could put together a portfolio of part-time jobs to bring in the equivalent of full-time employment. Haidee was also happy that she could find office work similar to that she had done previously at the Department of Social Security.

Obviously we didn't immediately announce that we were leaving as customers never like to feel that they are being 'deserted' but word eventually got out and many seemed genuinely sorry that we had decided to call time on the Brook. The three months seemed to fly by and I honestly can't remember whether trade was particularly good or bad during this time but do remember thinking that we had made the right decision. James Williams sent two couples to have a look at the premises. One couple was young and keen with some very good ideas and eminently suitable to be the next tenants. The other couple, Mr & Mrs Hugh Morgan-Salmon were considerably older than us and didn't seem to ask us any of the right questions. I don't need to tell you which couple James Williams chose.

I asked Frank Dunn, formerly of the Copper Coins to do our inventory and valuation for the ingoing which he did on 3 August (it was subject to adjustment on the day). The final valuation was fixtures and fittings £2923.50, kitchen equipment £107.50 and glassware,etc. £229.38, a total of £3260.38. This gave us an apparently reasonable profit on what we had paid six years before but taking into account the furniture, equipment, garden swings, etc. we had purchased over the years and inflation, it was almost certainly a loss. We made another loss on our last night of trading when we decided to thank all our regulars by charging the same prices that had applied on our first night in the Brook. *Worthington BB* was back to 29p a pint for one night only and a lot of it was drunk.

On change-over day, the Morgan-Salmons were pleasant enough but seemed more concerned with the comfort of their dog than the amount of beer stock I was leaving them with. On the other hand, I was keeping a very close eye on the stock take being done by the rep from James Williams and the inventory check on the glassware. One thing that really stuck in my mind was that when it proved apparently impossible to get a large settee up the stairs to the living accommodation, an immediate decision was made by Hugh to get a saw and hack the legs off. Everything was sorted in time for them to open at 11am. Fortunately unlike my predecessor George Dodd, I wasn't barred and was able to come back as a customer to continue playing for my darts team. I remember it being a very strange feeling the first time that I did.

The new landlord and landlady seemed to make very few changes in their first few months and after the initial curiosity factor period was over didn't seem to have any more trade than we had had. I wondered how long they would last but they were still there when a few years later James Williams eventually gave the place a very much needed interior re-vamp (and changed the exterior back to white and black). In the end Hugh died there but Joan Morgan-Salmon carried on to become the longest serving tenant since the almost legendary Gladys Hughes/Dillon.

So, there we were, Mum & Dad very happy in their new home in Hakin, making new friends and enjoying life generally. Sister Jennifer and her family settled in Neyland. Brother Nigel in a job he was enjoying and also living in Neyland in a new property he had purchased. Me giving my full attention to being Mr Town Clerk in Pembroke and with other part-time jobs in my sights and Haidee again working at the D.S.S. In Cherry Grove, Haverfordwest. Bill had been working at the Vehicle Licensing Office in Haverfordwest but transferred to the DVLC and moved to Swansea in October 1983. Douglas had left Milford Haven Grammar School at 16 but then signed up to a lengthy motor body repair course at Neyland Technical College which would lead him to his future career. Everybody happy and looking forward to having time to really enjoy Pembrokeshire then BANG – the bombshell landed.

The bomb that was to change our lives was dropped by the Local Government Boundary Commission. There had been consultations about the possibility of Pembroke and Pembroke Dock having separate councils. Pembroke Dock had been formalised as part of Pembroke as far back as 1835 when the Wards of Pembroke and Pennar were created within the Pembroke Borough Council. There was virtually no popular support for the creation of two councils to do the work that was being done satisfactorily by one with the virtual certainty of increased costs for very little, if any, benefit. Despite half of the members of Pembroke Town Council representing Pembroke Dock there was a clear majority for leaving things as they were.

Virtually no popular support, no public vote, but the Quango had spoken and one would become two. I began to speak privately to members and it soon became obvious that while Pembroke would possibly be ready to share a Town Clerk, Pembroke Dock probably would not and I was left with the certainty of dealing with all the hassle involved in splitting up the property and assets of such a long established Council with the virtual certainty of only having half of what was already a part-time job when it was all over or even the possibility of no job at all as both new councils would probably have to advertise for a new Clerk. This just wasn't viable and we soon decided that I would have to look for a new post and with a very heavy heart accepted that this would almost certainly be away from Pembrokeshire.

I applied for the post of Town Clerk at Newark-on-Trent in Nottinghamshire without success but I wasn't too unhappy as there seemed to be much more emphasis on tradition rather than actually doing things. Next I went for interview for the Clerk's job at Great Wyrley in Staffordshire said to be near Cannock Chase but in reality much nearer to Walsall. I was given a tour of the area prior to the interview and very quickly decided that it was not somewhere I wanted to live. I have no idea what it is like now but then, compared to Pembroke and Pembrokeshire, it was a complete dump. Having made up my mind that I didn't want the job, I decided that my interview strategy should be to slag the place off and find fault at every opportunity. This spectacularly backfired when they decided that I was, 'just the sort of man they were looking for'. I said that I would have to consult my wife before accepting. I telephoned the next day to say that they should appoint their second choice.

Next came Camberley Town Council in Surrey. I had a walk around town before the interview and a quick glance in a couple of estate agent's windows told me that there was no way that we could ever afford to move there. The price we had paid for Mum & Dad's bungalow just a few months before would just about have got us a caravan in this area. The interview was going well and I was about to be offered the job until, in fairness, I told them what the situation was and wondered whether they would be able to assist with house purchase. They were not amused, refused to pay my expenses and again I felt relieved that I had escaped them rather than feeling any sense of failure.

My next journey was to Thornbury, then in the 1970s abomination that was the County of Avon but later in South Gloucestershire. This was a pleasant, characterful market town but the Town Council ran a busy cemetery, playing fields with resident football teams, open spaces with play equipment and a community facility with meeting rooms, halls, stage and dressing rooms, none of which I had any experience of. But they were looking for someone who knew how to be a Town Clerk and ideally someone who knew something about licensed premises as the community centre had a bar so I thought I was in with a chance. The signs were good when following, a tour of the town, the candidates were given lunch with a number of Councillors in the skittle alley of the pub nearest the Council's offices (obviously part of the interview where one candidate showed few social graces and almost certainly eliminated himself). The reaction between the bar and waiting staff and some of the Councillors showed that they were regular customers – another good sign.

The interview went very well and afterwards the Town Clerk, George Excell, who was retiring after many years service said that he would telephone with the result after I got home that evening. I thought he winked at that point but couldn't be sure as he had a 'funny' eye. If it wasn't a wink it should have been because when the phone call came it was to tell me that the job was mine if I wanted it and of course I did. Property in Thornbury was (just) affordable and a flat attached to the Council's offices was made available while we looked at our leisure for somewhere to live. In a previous life, the offices had been a bakers shop and tearooms. My office would be what was once the tea room and we would live for several months 'above the shop'. I would start my new job towards the end of May 1984 and I have always denied the allegation that the only reason I got the the post was so that the Councillors wouldn't need to try to remember a new first name for their Clerk.

It was great that I had got a job that secured our future but we were leaving Pembrokeshire which we loved, a large number of friends that we had made over the years and of course, a fair chunk of my family. Mum & Dad were, as ever, fully supportive and appreciated that I had to go where the work was. I still felt a bit guilty however that having started the mass migration to West Wales we were now leaving behind those who had followed us. We received many good wishes from former fellow work colleagues, pub customers, officers of Dyfed County and South Pembrokeshire District Councils and friends generally. Probably the most surprising was the presentation of a clock in recognition of my work as Secretary of the Coastal Darts League.

One of my last duties as Pembroke Town Clerk was the Mayor making, civic lunch and Mayor's ball for Cllr. Derek Lloyd who would be the last of the six Mayors of Pembroke that I served. Derek, another lovely man, was Public Relations Officer at the *Texaco* Refinery and it would have been great to have done a full year with him. The next surprise was at the civic lunch. I had just performed the last part of my duty as toastmaster when Cllr. Don Kingdom, another man I got on very well with, stood up and gave me a speech of thanks and farewell. My successor had already been chosen and two retired police officers had been among the candidates interviewed so I was able to say in my response that I had come to Pembroke as a humble former PC to take on the work of two people, that it had taken an Inspector to replace me and a Chief Inspector didn't even get the job. The local press were out in force for my last meeting and I was photographed with the six Mayors I had served:- (left to right below) Ernie Morgan, Walford Davies, Charlie Thomas, Derek Lloyd, Rowena Thomas and Brian Phillips. I was presented with a framed engraving of Pembroke Castle and a silver tankard and left Pembroke Town Council with some very good memories

There must have been more last visits, last nights and last various things but they are forgotten in a blur. So just under seventeen years since we first saw Pembrokeshire and just over thirteen years since we had moved there, we were no longer residents but visits obviously continued. The County and its people will always have a place in my heart.

With my six Mayors pictured in the Courtroom (Now a museum) – Where did I get those trousers?

POST SCRIPT

Mum and Dad lived happily in Hakin for the rest of their lives. Dad died in January 2000 aged 89 and Mum in November 2002 aged 86. Both are now at rest with Gran Maud in Dale Cemetery.

Sister Jennifer still lives in Neyland having taken an active part in community life, especially the church and serving as a Neyland Town Councillor. Three of her six children still live in Pembrokeshire along with a fair proportion of her countless grandchildren and great grandchildren.

Brother Nigel married Pembrokeshire girl Janice Roberts in August 1985. Around a year later and very much out of the blue the firm he worked for re-located to Yate which is just nine miles away from Thornbury. As a result and despite his company's subsequent changes of name and location, he and his wife have lived just a few hundred yards away from me ever since.

Sister Margaret visited Pembrokeshire on a number of occasions but remained in Bedfordshire until years later when her husband's work took him to Filton and they moved to Staple Hill in Bristol. Their children Libby and Chris both emigrated to Australia and New Zealand. Maggie died in January 2017.

Son Bill moved from DVLC to Inland Revenue and married a Swansea girl. They later divorced and after some time working in Cheshire he is now a senior HMRC investigator based in Bristol and living happily in Yate with his second wife June. They love Pembrokeshire and hope to retire there.

Son Douglas moved with us to Thornbury and has his own home in the town. He has followed a career in automotive re-finishing and classic vehicle restoration and is now working locally.

Pembroke and Pembroke Dock Councils did finally split and Pembroke Dock elected its first Mayor in 1988. Two Councillors from my time there are still in office as I write – Cllr. Clive Collins in Pembroke and Cllr. Mrs Pam George who has been Mayor of Pembroke Dock seven times. Her father was Charlie Thomas who was one of my Mayors.

The Brook Inn, despite my numerous trips to Pembrokeshire, was not visited again by me until June 2019 when, with my sister, I found it much changed for the better and in the very capable hands of Jonny Pawlett (son of one of our old customers Glyn Pawlett) and his partner Sally Llewellin (granddaughter of John Llewellin of Bicton Farm our potato supplier). They had been there five years and seemed to me to be doing everything right but unfortunately following the enforced closure caused by the 2020 Covid-19 pandemic, the Brook didn't re-open and at the time of writing is for sale. It can only be hoped that it will remain a pub when a buyer is found.

I stayed with Thornbury Town Council until taking early retirement in 2001 to become Vice-President and then penultimate President of the Hearts of Oak Friendly Society based in Leicester and helping to oversee its merger with Reliance Mutual. During my time with the Council I managed projects including the purchase of a building and its conversion to a local museum, the acquisition and renovation of a former Magistrates Court to become a new Town Hall and community space, acquisition of land for additional open spaces, play areas and sports pitches, twinning with Bockenem in Germany and the first of many successful entries in the Britain in Bloom competition. On a voluntary basis I worked for the Lions, Christmas Lights Association, Sea Cadets and Royal British Legion.

Haidee worked for a number of years for Clerical Medical Insurance in Bristol and then as receptionist at Thornbury's Golf Centre. She too was and is active in the community. We separated in August 2008 but remain married. I still live in Thornbury, she is a few miles away in Wotton-Under-Edge.

The family (l to r) Me, Jennifer, Maggie and Nigel with Mum & Dad

OTHER BOOKS BY GEORGE JACKSON

All available at *Amazon*

MY FIRST FOUR LIVES – This autobiography covers the first 35 years of the author's life spanning the 1940s to 1970s. It provides a fascinating and humorous insight into growing up in Houghton Regis, Bedfordshire. Life at Dunstable Grammar School and working for the Meteorological Office in Bedfordshire, Hertfordshire and Berkshire at the very dawn of that organisation's computer age. His third and fourth lives as a Police Officer in Huntingdonshire and then Pembrokeshire provide a further fund of revelations and anecdotes. This is real social history but with a sense of fun, told by a skilful story-teller and well illustrated with some unique photographs.

LUTON TOWN F.C. - A SEASON BY SEASON HISTORY 1885-2018 – This book is what it says on the cover – a history but it is a personal view of that history. Every season is looked at in terms of stand-out events, comings and goings, great results and disasters, characters on and off the pitch and some of the author's personal memories. It tries to give statistics a personal dimension and hopefully contains more than a few facts and figures that the reader has either forgotten or had never ever known.

PLAYING WITH WORDS AND OTHER THINGS – Does just that. It is a Pick 'n' Mix of prose, poems, puns, posers, parables, parodies, paradoxes and piss-takes paraded in no particular order. There is some irony, a bit of euphony and a fair proportion of nostalgia (Although we are told that's not what it used to be). Hopefully, every page will bring a chuckle, a smile, a nod of agreement or at the very least just a groan.

PLAYING WITH WORDS AGAIN- A skilful mix of prose, puns, poems, parodies and parables delivers a nostalgic look at the past and the paradoxes, politics and pandemic of the present all woven together with timeless humour. From Marie Curie to Greta Thunberg, Amazin' Raisins to Shiitake mushrooms, Winston Churchill to Keir Starmer, Poets Laureate to Jack & Jill and from constipation to Covid-19, there are endless ways to make you smile.

MY PEAKY BLINDER UNCLE- A true story. It was family legend that the author's father had an uncle by marriage who had got into trouble with a gang in Birmingham, had been shot at and had therefore run away from time to time to join a Circus and ride the 'Itchy Mule'. The truth is much more legendary and Uncle Billy Beach wasn't just shot at, he was wounded several times, he wasn't just in trouble with a gang, he led one as part of the infamous Garrison Lane Vendetta and he was just as likely to have been in Winson Green Prison as away with the Circus. In an attempt to end the vendetta he emigrated to Canada but at the outbreak of WW1 almost immediately volunteered and fought and was wounded at the 2nd Battle of Ypres with the Royal Canadian Highlanders. Back in the UK for treatment and on return to Canada, trouble followed him around until peace broke out when he returned to his wife and family in 1925. Quite a character but perhaps not all bad.

Printed in Great Britain
by Amazon